dust bunnies
a memoir

tommy womack

Edited by Brian J. Buchanan
Copy-edited and proofed by Chris Erikson

Photography by Alan Messer

Cover design and illustrations by Brad Talbott
Typeset and layout by Keata Brewer

ISBN 978-0-692-18057-0

Tommywomack.com
tommywomack@bellsouth.net
PO Box 41954
Nashville, TN 37204

Many thanks, as always, to the toppermost of the poppermost, Richard Courtney. Thanks to Matt Byrd, Charlie Kington, John Hiatt, Maryglenn McCombs, Russ Riddle, Peter Cooper, Mandy Haynes, Kent Agee, Chuck Beard, Garry Tallent, Will Kimbrough, Michael Gray, Marshall Chapman, Todd Snider, Warner Hodges, Art L, Teresa Medeiros and Laurie and Steve Gregory for all their help. Posthumous loving thanks to Ann Tucker.

With all my love
this book is dedicated to
my wife, Beth, and my son, Nathan,
without whom I wouldn't have a wife or a son.

contents

We drag our lives around like screaming children.

— Joe Bolton

introduction:

the things you learn in the back of a car

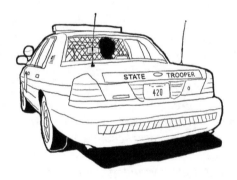

I always wondered what the world looked like from the back seat of a police cruiser. Now I know. Right now I'm thanking sweet Jesus in Heaven that I have Xanax, marijuana and Wild Turkey in my system, otherwise I don't think I would tolerate this situation nearly as well as I am right now. What's lost on me at the moment is the fact that it's that cocktail of chemicals that has me in this back seat to begin with. If it weren't for those things, I'd be on the interstate by now, driving home from a great gig. And it WAS a great gig. Standing ovation, the whole nine yards. Moved a lot of merch. Got a cool festival T-shirt. A great night. And it's still great, in an odd way. It's great because I have a good buzz, and let's be frank; that's all that matters.

My mind isn't saying, "Ooh, this is really fucked up and I'm really in trouble." It's saying, "Hey, this is a new experience that will make a great story; and if I was ever going to be butt-raped by Bubba in a soundproof cell, this is exactly the buzz I'd want to have when it happens."

It's Memorial Day weekend, 2012, and Tennessee is warm and humid even at midnight. We like it that way. We tell Yankees, You think this is hot, come back in August, we'll show you hot. This? This is nice. My new festival T-shirt isn't even sweaty, and this cruiser is air-conditioned. What more could a fucked-up musician possibly want?

There's just one thing I really don't like. Wait, two things. First are these handcuffs. I've seen enough criminals on television complaining that their cuffs are too tight, and how uncomfortable it is to be cuffed behind your back so that you're essentially sitting on your hands in the back seat of the cruiser and the metal of the cuffs is biting into your wrist bones. I'd always had contempt for those criminals. You deserve it, you piece of shit. What do you expect after killing all those nurses? Now I have a new empathy. It hurts. But, again, I'm lucky: if I weren't fucked up out of my mind, think how bad it would hurt then. Thank God for chemicals that get me into trouble and make the trouble feel good at the same time. Drugs are great. Everyone should try them.

Secondly, that little piece of paper taped up to the Plexiglas wall between the officers in the front seat and me back here. It's about two inches tall by three or four inches wide, and it says: "And I will strike down upon thee with great vengeance and furious anger those who would attempt to poison and destroy my brothers. And you will know my name is the Lord when I lay my vengeance upon thee. – Ezekiel 25:17."

Now that's not cool, I think. I don't need to see that. How many perps have seen that, from my vantage right here? The paper is brown and the cellophane tape is yellowed, and no one has been able to rip it down, or lunge forward and eat it, because of the cuffs, and the tightest seat belt ever. I wonder if the cops know about Samuel Jackson reciting that very verse before icing people in Pulp Fiction. *I doubt it. The Christian music blaring from the radio tells me they might not even know who Quentin Tarantino is. I believe in God and I believe He hates Christian music as much as I do. I spend a lot of time on the road, and as I'm flipping the radio left of the dial I can tell the Christian station in two notes. It always sounds like Coldplay with a really, really happy lead singer. The radio is all New Testament happy happy joy joy. That piece of paper is Old Testament Yahweh that will kick you into the middle of next month, pudknocker! I wonder which side of the fence the cops sit on, liturgically, or if their minds plumb such channels at all.*

I'm starting to not like them. They were courteous enough when I was stumbling through their stupid human tricks, but now that I'm in the back seat and they're up front, it's like I don't exist. They don't make conversation with me, it just puts a guy off. It's not like I'm asking them to go through Wendy's or anything. I'm starting to see why mother-rapers and father-stabbers don't like the constables that cross their paths. The way they treat you like a common criminal. I also don't like how the guy is driving now. He's violating every speed law in the county, slowing down for curves and then gunning it in the straightaways. He's saying, I'm a cop, and I don't have to follow the laws of the road. Arrogance! If I were doing coke right now I'd give him a piece of my mind.

Someday years later I'll be typing and thinking about how this was a turning point, how when I came out of my fog in the morning, waking up on a cold cement floor in a drunk tank in Bumfuck, Tennessee, I thought things might have to change now. I'd lived a great rock 'n' roll life. Almost died once or twice, but you know. Shit happens. I'd always gotten away with it. Close shaves are the spice of life, right? Well this time I didn't get away with it. And this time I'm going to fork out a grand for a lawyer, have more jail hanging over my head, pay fines and court costs, and find how all this scuttles my enjoyment of Lockup *marathons on MSNBC. I'm going to have to stop using a dysfunctional upbringing as an excuse to stay numb, going to have to get help, going to have to get typing, going to have to spell out this life and let it be enough for once.*

call to worship

The best thing about Attention Deficit Disorder is it never bothers you too long at any one time. *Badumpum.* Thank you, I'll be here all week.

* * * * * *

It's hard to think of my mother as a child but she was one once. And one day she was sitting at the table minding her own business. Her father was sitting there minding his own business too, when out of nowhere he just looked at her and said, "You know, you're about the ugliest thing I've ever seen in my life."

He said just those words to his little daughter, stood up from the table and walked right out the front door of the house.

Mom, not being Mom yet and still a little girl, kind of laughed startled for a second, because surely to God he was kidding. She waited for him to pop his face back around the door with a big smile and then run back to the table and hug on her neck and surely to God he would because surely to frickin' God he was *kidding*. Apparently he wasn't kidding, and he didn't come back in the house.

And whenever he *did* come back there was no explanation or anything—like it had never happened. It happened, believe me. If I heard that story once, I heard it a blue million times.

That incident broke my mother's little-girl heart. She never got over that.

Lorene Virginia Waters Womack.
Rene Womack, to most people.
Mom.

* * * * * *

I knew Papa Waters; he wasn't an evil man and Mom never had an ugly day in her life, so your guess is as good as mine why he'd say such a thing.

But at least with Mom I have a clue when and why her life became a depressed person's life. I know what happened. Believe me, I know already.

When and where Dad's life went to shit—and how and why—I have no clue. What he ever told me of his life I could write down with a Sharpie on the back of a prescription.

* * * * * *

James Carson Womack.
The Reverend J. C. Womack.
Dad.
Back in the '60s when I was a little kid, he wore horn-rimmed glasses like everybody wore in all the Kennedy assassination pictures and Beatle press conferences, and they suited him.

In his prime he preached a sermon every Sunday morning, often two, and sometimes three. He shook hands with every parishioner who came out the front door after the church service.

He'd give everybody his grin. I have his grin, a big wide Joker grin that looks like a comedy mask. When Dad smiled big like that he looked like an idiot. So do I.

When we got back home, he loosened his tie, got into his recliner, kicked it back, fired up a Camel, got Mom to bring him a glass of sweet tea, and you didn't get between him and the TV if the house was on fire.

Church folks always thought Brother Womack was the funniest, knee-slappingest preacher you ever could meet. They never saw him sitting in that recliner with his glasses reflecting ice-blue television flickers night after night. He was a preacher moonlighting as a potted plant and nobody knew it but Mom and us three kids.

Dad watched hours of television at a stretch. We all did. You couldn't blame us. Television was much better than our real lives. I'd be watching Mike Brady give his boys warm, fatherly advice. And Dad would fart real loud with no change of facial expression. He'd push his upper dentures forward with his tongue so as to look momentarily like a Neanderthal tracking Lee Harvey Oswald in '60s horn-rims. Then he'd suck them back in. Then he'd pick his nose like he'd left a goddam nickel up there.

I'd be sitting there watching TV and feeling majorly ripped-off. Little Bobby Brady, played by a boy named Mike, got the warm, congenial Mike Brady for a dad—who was played by a gay guy named Bobby. And that was better than reality. Thanks, God.

* * * * * *

Was he preoccupied? Writing sermons in his head? Spinning lurid thoughts? Quietly convinced he was the King of Spain? I couldn't tell you. I have no idea.

All I can tell you is he left the Christmas lights up until July one year. We had Christmas lights on the gutter for seven, maybe eight months. He took them down on a steamy July day in Kentucky. I stood in my short pants and flip-flops in the front yard and watched.

It was a red-letter day, like any other of the sporadic occasions when Dad would come out of his stupor long enough to do something complicated like taking a fucking ladder out of the fucking garage, climbing up in his church pants and taking the goddam Christmas lights down. I think I was eight.

* * * * * *

This is a very profane book, and I apologize for that. I'm actually not that big a fan of profanity, but those are the words that come from my angry core. I don't choose them, they bubble up and shoot out like magma. It doesn't help that I spent a lot of my formative years reading *Creem* magazine, the greatest rock 'n' roll periodical of all time and sopping wet with filthy language. Factor in that I've spent over a quarter century playing rock 'n' roll, and there you have it: I have a dirty mouth.

When *Cheese Chronicles* came out in 1995, Mom was torn between being very proud of me and being appalled by my gutter language. The first thing she did when she sat down to read it was to get some Liquid Paper, so as to blot out the bad words. She wanted to do that so that the relatives in Arkansas wouldn't have to read such a book, reckoning I guess that the relatives would all read only this particular copy, passing it around.

Trouble was that Mom's hands shook so badly that, as she drew white lines across expletives, she obliterated text above and below the offending word. Every once in a while she'd turn the page before the substance dried, leaving random blotches here and there, pages sticking together, etc. In the end it was unreadable, and Mom abandoned her efforts halfway through, because by then the relatives had already seen virgin copies free of prettifying.

Around the age of 45 I figured something out about why Mom was so riled by bad language. Where she came from was a community of people so poor and so downtrodden that there were only two things they had control over to separate themselves from poor white trash: whether you went to church, and what words you let come out of your mouth. That's it. No other factors. When that hit me, I finally understood where Mom was coming from. I on the other hand grew up with indoor plumbing, air conditioning and more than one change of clothes, and I currently live in a pleasant suburb, so I'm somewhat liberated from the constraints Mom felt. At least that's what I tell myself.

I take the Lord's name in vain here and there, and I do worry about it. Where I come from, that's a big no-no. Where I draw the line is that there is a god and there is God, and so spelling goddamn in all lower case letters lets me squeak by on a technicality while enjoying the cadence of the syllables. I know it's splitting hairs, but my lawyer says he can get me off with time served if this goes to trial.

* * * * * *

In fifth grade, I started blinking my eyes a lot. Hard blinks where my eyes would scrunch up and my brow would expand. Then I started weirdly stretching the skin on the front of my neck up to under my chin, over and over. A substitute teacher one day wasn't hip to how I was and gave me the stink eye because she thought I was making faces at her. It got worse instead of better. I started jerking my head forward spasmodically, often in tandem with a blink. It continued that way my entire junior high and senior high lives with no one in the world knowing why I was pulling this crazy shit. It was a pain in the ass then. And it's a pain in the ass now.

Over my whole life, I've kept up my old riffs and expanded to quiet grunting noises in my throat and clicking my tongue against a back molar until I wear a sore on it. The head jerking comes and goes but my neck muscles are tight as hell forever from the stress of it. Old Faithful, the blinking, remains with me all day every day. I've had problems with conjunctivitis, my upper eyeballs being inflamed from eyelids rubbing against them with such consistence and velocity for decades. There has been no one since I was a young child for whom my tics have not made up part of their first impression of me.

No one in Madisonville back then had ever heard of Tourette's. Mom would harp at me to stop it. Dad didn't. (Dad might never have frickin' *noticed*.) But it defined me. Man, that Womack, he ain't right. Hell NO I won't go out on a date with him! Hey, let's blink back at him!

As I blinked and jerked and tap danced through the minefield of puberty, I thought a lot about how to deal with the most vociferous of the Bund rally sophomores and juniors and seniors, the ones who ran that school and thought I was crazy, and that's when I started my long trek up the mountain of humor.

I listened to Steve Martin records, and Cheech & Chong and George Carlin records, Bill Cosby records; I recorded entire Monty Python episodes onto audiocassettes, and I listened to them all like they were music. I didn't just learn the jokes (and recite them obnoxiously at school, like I did too often), I listened for the cadence, the timing, the elements of surprise and incongruity, and the ultimate aim: articulating something everybody thinks about but dares not say. By senior year, my budding comic guise produced humor about 20 percent of the time. To pad my act, I threw in a dollop of Dadaism. I learned that if you don't have something funny to say to an asshole in the hallway between classes, then say something oblique that makes no sense at all, and walk on. Some will think it's a joke they didn't get. Maybe a good joke. And maybe they're the ignorant ones. That was my goal anyway. You fuck with me about my blinking, I'll fuck you up good like a puppy dressed up for Thanksgiving!

* * * * * *

I've had a joyous life and a bleak, hopeless life. Meds and the love of a good woman have saved me. That and having an audience. I write my little songs and my little books and make my modest-selling records, write my columns and articles, and I have a small but devoted following. I'm an acquired taste. You have to love insanity and honesty. I lay it all out there and it makes some people uncomfortable. Not everybody wants that in music, and I understand, but love songs are not my forte. Nor dance ditties. I write songs about religion, the Replacements, therapists, fish sticks, yellow cling peaches, camping on acid, cheap sex, overdosing, Cheetah Chrome, my family, Jesus, alcoholism, Kentucky, Martin Luther slinging his own shit at a vision of Satan, and an all-consuming fear of dying poor. It saves the live show that a lot of the songs are funny, if you like what I think is funny.

* * * * * *

Everybody loses his or her emotional virginity, usually in childhood, when life hits you hard, and if you don't bounce back, you become a new person. Mom had it at the table with Papa Waters; I had it in high school, the worst four years of my life. Nearly forty years later I'm still pissed off and there's nobody to sue. I worked at a car wash in my twenties and came in one day on acid with big black eyes like a great white shark. I was laughing my ass off in customers' faces and whacking drumbeats on seat cushions with the vacuum wand, bent over in a blind mental hernia wondering what the hell I was doing with my life, and that was a pleasant, well-adjusted day compared to high school.

* * * * * *

Rednecks are like dogs. You either smell like family or they'll keep pissing on you 'til you do.

* * * * * *

I live life like a pinball, four or five paragraphs at a time. It's like the Vonnegut story where every five minutes a big bell rings very loudly and scrambles everybody's thoughts. Forty years ago in Kentucky we didn't have Ritalin. We didn't even have ADHD. You just "weren't right."

What you might call ADHD, I call growing up when sugar was cool, when kids like me ate repeated bowls of Sugar Crisp, Sugar Smacks, Sugar Pops, and my favorite, Cheerios with four heaping teaspoons of sugar. Now they sell Super *Golden* Crisp and Super *Golden* Pops, and my whole life's a disorder there's a drug for, as if I'm not already doing enough as it is. Not to mention that "Super Golden Crisp" is a pussy-ass name.

* * * * * *

Christianity is a religion named after its founder, Jesus Christ, a man whose name was neither Jesus nor Christ, who never founded a religion and don't get me started.

But if you're Christian from the dirt up, you won't kill yourself. No matter how bad things ever get you won't take that route, because to do so is to fry in a lake of fire for eternity like a slice of country ham. Nasty image. Negative reinforcement with hair on it. But in a world without antidepressants it'll keep your ass alive.

* * * * * *

Madisonville, Kentucky.

"The Best Town on Earth."

That's the town motto and it's perfect. No other one-syllable words could evoke the crackling wit that runs through that town like cold blood through a roadkill possum. "The Best Town on Earth." Peppy, one-syllable words, and an outrageous lie. Madisonville isn't even the best town in Kentucky, much less the planet.

About 18,000 short-haired, Christian coal miners lived there when I was a kid, watching television there, sending their kids to school there and working the earth with big shovels biting into the rolling hills of Western Kentucky.

If you haven't had business there, you've never been there. It's not on the way to anything anyone's ever judged worth seeing. The land is not quite flat like the western edge where the Ohio and Mississippi meet, and it's not the dirt-poor batshit hillbilly mountains to the east. It's not the northern bluegrass horse country; it's not anything at all.

That motto is actually just the official one. The real one is "Kiss my ass," and you say "ass" like "aeiss," halfway between "ace" and "ice" but really neither one. And if you weren't raised here, you'll never say it right.

I was delivering ice to a Kwik Pik Market in the summer of 1981, filling the outside box with bags of ice, and as the driver and I got back in the truck to go to our next stop, I noticed the graffiti spray-painted on the cinderblock wall above the ice chest in big letters. AC/CD.

I can understand spelling "there" when you mean "their" and even, God help us, apostrophizing plurals, but fucking up AC/DC? That's beyond the pale. The Best Town on Earth, *and if yew dont lik my speling yew can kiss my aeiss!*

* * * * * *

It's May 23rd, 1990. I'm in the Government Cheese van, slumped in a back seat with four other miscreants who, as often as not, don't like each other anymore. My hair is long, tangled and greasy, I haven't showered since Pittsburgh, I'm wearing the same yellow frilly tuxedo shirt I've had on for three days, or maybe it's four days. I have my Peter Buck black vest on, my jeans with the hole in the crotch, my black Reeboks with holes in both toes and red sock toes peeking out. It's workable at this point just to wear stage clothes all the time. Cuts down on the thinking.

We've stopped in Bowling Green at 11 a.m. after an all-night drive from wherever the fuck, just long enough to put clean underwear in our bags and stop at the Minute Mart to check our PO box and get some beer. Then it's off to Ruston, Louisiana. I think. The Minute Mart is next to the Tender Touch Auto Wash, where Viva, Billy Mack and I work when we're home. Successful rock stars. Yay rah.

I got something addressed to me in the mail. It's an envelope with what feels like a greeting card inside. I hem and haw over whether to open it first or open a beer first. Beer wins. Hiss goes the bottle cap, which I throw forward to hit the windshield and irritate whoever's up front. I take a hit off my pot pipe, then I have a mind-clearing sip of pre-noon beer and open my mail.

It's an invitation to my tenth high school reunion. Jesus H. Willy Wonka. I lean back with my beer and think as somebody turns the Replacements up on the cassette deck. I think how only one type of people stage high school reunions: the ones who had a good time then, also known as "assholes." One thing is cool, though. The Buffy or Biff who addressed this envelope knew to send it c/o Government Cheese. My reputation is spreading.

My nickname in the band is The Acknowledger, because I acknowledge. That means that every once in a while, as we travel, usually after a lung-bursting toke or five, I reach forward, turn the music down and hold forth out of nowhere and apropos of nothing. If the others dig it, they snap their fingers like beatniks in a coffee bar.

"I don't go to high school reunions," I intone like Antony burying Caesar, "I don't go to high school reunions for the same reason that Vietnamese Boat People don't get together in Atlantic City and reminisce about salty sun blisters and eating raw plankton. 'Ooh! Le Duc! You look great! Lip look much better now!'"

I take a swig and muse for a second, and then before someone can turn the Replacements back up, I start in again.

"It could be a nice evening. Surprisingly so! I might discover these people as they really are now: nice people, grown-up and no longer taking courtesy as a weakness. I might have a wonderful conversation with a sparkling 28-year-old lady who was a self-loading howitzer bitch on wheels ten years ago, and we'll discover each other as we are now, and maybe part of my heart will be healed. And maybe Hermann Goering could have had a second career in the '50s as a wacky sitcom neighbor, if he'd played his cards right at Nuremberg. I wouldn't get near that evening with tongs. I don't want to sound bitter."

Silence. Joe snaps his fingers. Skot turns the 'Mats back up. I slump back. Life goes on.

2

great vituperous gouts

Sunday, November 20, 2011

Got in at 3:30 this morning from Johnson City. Five-hour drive back from the gig. I wanted to wake up in my own bed on my birthday. Listened to Coast to Coast AM, alone in the magic darkness, signal fading in and out, crinkly voices of ghost hunters, UFO buffs, conspiracy theorists and old guys from Montana who are out of their tiny little minds. I was born 49 years ago today. At 1:30 a.m., November 20, 1962.

Scott Willis says I'm the most insane person he's ever met who has his life together. Todd Snider says I'm the only person he's met in Nashville who's crazier than he is. In high school, goddam everybody signed my yearbook, "To the craziest person I know!" I have never, not once in my life, done anything trying to be crazy.

Whenever I've taken my pants off onstage, it's because that's exactly what the show needed at that moment. When I drafted my band to help me shave my head at 4 a.m. in a Marietta Motel 6, it was because I thought it was something fun we could all do together.

I'm an alcoholic and drug addict who's smoked enough dope to put 15 Mexican families through college. I'm always trying to get clean but I have so many habits that it's hard to keep up with them all. Right now I've been alcohol-free for 27 days. And I haven't smoked pot in—let me see, here—two hours, more or less.

I was asleep on the couch by 4:30 a.m., since Nathan was sleeping in my spot next to Beth and I didn't feel like picking a fight with an adolescent zombie. He's 14 years old already. Seems like yesterday I was changing diapers. I woke up at noon with him standing over me, cocking his Nerf gun next to my ear. Four cups of coffee later, I helped him with his homework: drafting an accurate floor plan of our house, and writing a two-page report on the ancient Greek torsion catapult, all while watching the Titans lose to the Falcons. This is my life. There are worse ones. I've had them.

* * * * * *

Mom grew up dirt-poor in the Arkansas Delta during the Great Depression. It was a family of sharecroppers, and Mom was out in the field picking cotton as soon as she was able to hold the burlap sack. Mama and Papa Waters and their daughter worked on a different plantation every season, always moving all they owned to another farm. When Mom married Dad she was 16 years old and had lived in a different home every year of her life: 16 years, 16 different shacks.

* * * * * *

Monday, November 21, 2011

Pot is salt and pepper for the brain; if you feel good, it'll make you feel better; if you feel bad, it'll flood your body with the ice-cold piss of Satan. I have a serious anger problem. If I get started being mad it's hard for me to stop. And that's where the weed's been useful all these years. They don't call it an attitude adjustment for nothing. I'd be so pissed at somebody in the band and not feel like going onstage and faking smiles in that person's direction, but three tokes later I'd be as happy as a spring lamb, yukking it up and rocking faces off.

Pot's always taken my mind away from that eighth-grader inside of me, the benchwarmer, the guy who couldn't climb the rope in gym class, the guy who was radioactive to girls until he put a six-string electric penis around his torso. Factor in the creativity thing: I was high yesterday and wrote like the wind; today I'm straight and it's pulling teeth. I can always write on pot, prose or lyrics, doesn't matter. There are songs in pot. I'm sorry, there just are.

And that's what I'm in this town for: songs. I'm in Nashville. We make some of the best music in the world right here every day. We also spew rancid, prefab sonic putrescence into the face of a defenseless public. We're talking shit. I've smoked a lot of weed trying to figure out how to come up with some million-dollar dreck that makes me puke, but it's hard to play guitar and hold your nose at the same time.

Two and a Half Men is coming on.

* * * * * *

Playing acoustic guitar and singing all by yourself in a bar full of people is like swatting at surf on the beach with a badminton racquet. You play. They drink, talk and laugh. You play louder. They get louder. You consider killing yourself.

Owensboro, Kentucky, somewhere around September of 2010. A friend had found me a gig at a frat bar for $200 and beggars can't be choosers: $200 is $200. It was packed in there, and not because of me. In all directions were Sigma Chis and Kappa Deltas guzzling draft beer out of plastic glasses. You really just wanted to pull out a flame-thrower and spray the room. I had two choices: (a) play the gig, or (b) drink lots of vodka and play the gig. I had at least three good belts before I even took the stage, such as there was one (a little raised place in a corner). My plaintive, neutered-coyote singing splashed against the drunk Greek ocean's roar. And the louder the ocean, the drunker I got.

A frat plebe bum-rushed me, red-faced, with one shirttail hanging out. "Hey, man, play 'Wagon Wheel' and I'll sing it!" I looked at him and said "Sure," as a little trickle of vomit rose over my bottom lip and ran down my chin. Did we play it? I've no clue. What I remember next is getting my pay at the end of the night (what was left of it after my tab), and the owner saying, "We think we should call you a taxi. Is there anywhere in town tonight you can stay?"

I picked up my guitar case and lurched a little in the direction of gravity. "Ma'am," I said, "I'm a musician." I wheeled and veered out the front door, threw my guitar into the trunk of my car, hunched over with my hands on my knees like a defensive end, shuddered and vomited great vituperous gouts of vodka, rage and digestive business from the southernmost alimentary zip code, and then I drove the two hours home.

* * * * * *

The world needs another singer-songwriter like it needs more second-hand smoke. My head is so far up my ass I can taste my own gall bladder. Those stories and Ron's forecast at 10.

* * * * * *

Wednesday, November 23, 2011

Today was a blessedly brief day at work. Thanksgiving. I only had to work three hours but got paid for my whole five, so that's what I'm thankful for today, that and for never having killed anyone with my car.

I work only five hours a day at my day job. It's all any of us coders do, because the work is so tedious and mentally exhausting. When I interviewed for the job, I soft-pedaled the whole ADD thing, and now it's come to bite me in the ass.

I work for Vanderbilt Medical Center reading patient complaints against doctors and staff, densely written gripes from forwarded emails that you have to read from the bottom up. I'm one of a dozen worker bees who slog through this crap, making copy-pasted bullet points and coding them according to the 34 different categories of complaint. A problem with treatment is a 13, making the patient wait is a 26, breach of confidentiality is a 7, poor communication skills is a 2. If it were any duller it would be Eric Clapton.

I hate Vanderbilt's guts. I've worked four different places there over the last 15 years. I hate every brick, every squirrel. A colorless bastion of sober neckties, weak smiles and fluorescent lights; 18,000 people work there and are divided into three groups: those with PhDs who are deeply fulfilled using their intellects to the fullest, those who would be living bland, paper-pushing lives no matter where they were and don't really think about it, and those like me who walk around campus wondering which tree branch might hold a rope and take my weight.

* * * * * *

I saw a scene in a movie once that nailed the music industry. It's in *Dumb and Dumber,* when Jim Carrey asks Lauren Holly if there's a chance for romance between the two of them. She replies, "If you were the last man on the planet, and I were the last woman, and it was up to the two of us to repopulate the planet for the future of mankind, then under those circumstances, I *might* consider it." Carrey furrows his dullard brow. Then his eyes grow big, a smile steals over his face, and he exclaims, "In other words . . . there's a CHANCE!"

cupcakes and pubic misfires

It is Friday, October 15, 1976, Madisonville, KY, 9:13 p.m. CST. There is a smell of popcorn, hot dogs and grass, newly mown and cool in the fall. Bugs dance around the great high floodlights and the marching band plays big, blurty and whiter than the Queen. My shoes are wet from dew, from walking around and around the football field. You don't sit in the bleachers in ninth grade, you walk around, bump into other people, see things. I'm staring a hole through her. She's as skinny as a little sapling but that's all right. All I need is an impossibly cute face and I can get lost. Short brown hair, freckles, a face like Mrs. Kotter. She's in black jeans, black shirt, black jacket; I would say she looks like Emma Peel but I'm only 13 and haven't seen The Avengers *yet. She's with several other girls: her sister Shala, Tammy Rogers, some others. They know I'm there, behind them. Helen Keller would have known I was there. Wherever they go, all around the football field, I'm ten yards away, looking like I'm doing something else. If Tina shimmies 40 feet up a phone pole, I'll be up that pole right behind her, looking around like it's the most natural thing in the world to be clinging to a phone pole like a three-toed sloth.*

* * * * * *

There's a part of my brain that plays old tapes from high school 24 hours a day, and they're like old cassettes played too much—especially the worst bits, the most horrible memories—rewound and replayed over and over, thousands of times. They're memories left out on the dashboard in the sun. The tapes in my head from that era are so damaged from use, it's hard to remember anything anymore the way it really happened.

* * * * * *

My grandfather Kit Carson Womack appears in the 1890 Census as a small child, disappears for the turn of the century, then shows back up as a young man in 1910. His parents both died at the same time somehow, and left five orphaned brothers who raised each other on the Oklahoma prairie, like some demon hybrid of *The Grapes of Wrath* and *Lord of the Flies.* They didn't grow up suave and mannerly.

Pa Kit had six kids, two wives in succession and a farm in Beebe, Arkansas. I've never heard anything good said about the man, but then again I never heard anyone talk about him but Mom. Dad told me his name once and dick else. I sat on his lap once my first Christmas, but I don't remember it. The only time I actually remember seeing him was at my first funeral and his last. That was 1967. I was four.

* * * * * *

There is no Christian euphemism for "flaming cunt."

That's as rude as English gets, and no Christian dialect goes that deep into the purgative trenches. Good Christians will furrow their brows and rack their skulls looking for something along the lines of "flaming cunt," and come up bupkus every time. When that sentiment applies to someone and you can't express it, polyps form on your soul. "Bless your heart" is as close as you'll come. The southern "aloha." It means whatever the hell you want it to.

And if you asked her about Pa Kit, Mom would wrinkle her kindly Christian brow, looking for a nice way to put it.

* * * * * *

I can remember Mom always having orange Knox gelatin drink in the house. When I was a young boy and she'd be feeding a family of five on 10 to 20 or 30 1972 dollars a week, no matter what, she got that Knox gelatin. "For strong healthy NAILS," it said. It took me years to realize

Mom never did her nails. She drank the stuff to keep the ulcers down—
the ones on her tongue, her throat, her lips. I get those ulcers too.

* * * * * *

When Mom met Dad at a party, she was 15 and he was 20. He was
leaning against a post on the front porch, crying his eyes out over his
dead mother. I can't imagine my Dad ever shedding a tear for anything
or anybody, but that's how he was behaving when she first met him. He
was being somebody I can't even comprehend.

They courted. He was charming as shit, witty, smiling like an idiot
all the time.

One day while they were walking down a leafy dirt road, he quoted
the only Shakespeare he knew to her.

"Y'know, Rene, Shakespeare said, 'All the world's a stage and we's
all just actors on it.'"

* * * * * *

Don't ask me why the two most churchgoing people I've ever known
got married in a general store, with a justice of the peace, but they did.

It was August 19, 1939. Dad was 21. Mom was 16.

I once asked Uncle Robert why they didn't get married in a church,
and Robert just said, in his laconic Arkansas way, "Well, Tom, back
then, when it was time to get married, it was time to get married." And
that's as far into my parents' sex life as I ever want to travel.

First Papa Waters calls her a dogface when she's five, and now the
bridal day that every girl dreams of is a walk down the aisle—between
the cornmeal on the right and smoked hams on the left, while other
people buy gum and use the bathroom. All because it was "time to get
married."

As a little girl's life began at a table in a sharecropper's shack, her
married life began in a general store.

* * * * * *

The newlywed Womacks stayed at a cousin's house that night. All their
friends threw a shivaree and filled their bed with leaves. They spent a
few minutes getting them all out of the bed and then, there they were.

Mr. and Mrs. James Carson Womack. Alone in a room. Mom was
already more alone that she realized.

She was a 16-year-old girl. She didn't know what to do. She didn't know how the man who said "all the world's a stage" had just stepped off of it forever. The idiot grin was gone, along with most of the guy she married.

He sat down on the foot of the bed in frowning silence; he removed his shoes and then his socks. Then he pulled out a pocketknife and he started digging at one of his toes, as if his blushing bride were not even in the room.

She stood there.

He dug.

She stood there some more.

He dug.

She went to the bathroom. She came out. He was digging.

It went on for maybe fifteen minutes.

She changed into her nightgown, got into bed and lay there looking at his silent back, clearing her throat once or twice. And she went to sleep. That was her wedding night.

* * * * * *

Sixty-six years after Mom and Dad's honeymoon, I was a wildly insecure 43-year-old man, losing my hair, rail thin, pale, out of shape, playing volleyball in Joe Elvis's pool on Memorial Day weekend, 2005.

Joe Elvis was the drummer in my first band, Government Cheese, and one of my best friends. He had a nice house and a pool. I was ever mindful that all my cool friends had nicer, cleaner houses than the one I've provided for my own family.

I left the party early, in a depressed condition, leaving my wife and son there to catch a ride home later on. I went home and lay in bed, staring up at the weird shadows around the ceiling fan. And I wondered how I was ever going to give my family a life with a swimming pool. How the hell am I going to provide a proper Brady Bunch life on two-bit gigs, double-digit royalty checks and shit-ass day jobs? Everything looked hopeless and I was ashamed.

A week later we visited our friends the Kennadys, who lived in a subdivision with its own pool for residents. Into the waters we went again, my wife, Beth, our seven-year-old son, Nathan, and me. Something was better this weekend than last weekend. I had all my worries but Nathan was so happy playing in that pool, playing with me, other kids, Mom, that I got on his wavelength a bit. I was lifting him up in the air so he would come down with a big splash. Twice he exclaimed, "I love you, Daddy!" That was a happy kid. And for a minute or two here and there, so was I for a bright shining moment.

A month or so later I was in Texas on Todd Snider's tour bus, playing bass in his band. One afternoon the pot was hitting me bad and making me feel sad. I had to write something, anything, to get that feeling out of my system. I found a piece of paper and a pen, and in short order I wrote a testament to fear, love and living in the now. And it would become far and away the most popular and requested song in my entire solo career.

Nice Day

It's been a nice day, we all went swimming
Me and my sweetheart and our boy
It's been a nice day, we had a good time
The sun was shining and life was joy

It was at a friend's house, we got invited
We can't afford a swimming pool ourselves
Our beds are unmade, our bills are half-paid
But we got beans up on the shelves

I'm 43 now, my hair is going
I got a shaky sense of self-esteem
But in that water, that smile on my boy's face
For a moment life was not a bad dream

It's been a nice day, we all went swimming
I love you Daddy, he said that twice
Nothing got broken, no one got sunburned
I never freaked out, it was nice

I worry often, I live in terror
Of what life might have in store
I've got this vision, working at Mapco
Making change when I'm 64

I'll be an old man, I'll have had a good time
I'll have, God willing, my boy and my girl
And then I'll die, and go to God's house
Singing "take me from this world."

It's been a nice day, we all went swimming
Me and my sweetheart and our boy

That paper stayed folded up in the back pocket of my jeans for the rest of the tour. And when I got home a few nights later, I came into the house to find Nathan watching *Toy Story* in the living room. "Hey, buddy," I said, "I wrote a song and you're in it. Would you like to hear it?" He shrugged and said, "Sure."

We went out on our small front porch with my guitar and the lyrics and sat next to each other, looking at the moon. I had not written a tune yet, so I bluffed it. I started just playing the same three chords over and over again. There was no bridge, no chorus, just me winging it.

I sang the song all the way through, sat the guitar down and then it was just me, the boy and the crickets, and the streetlight, and the moon. Nathan scooted over closer to me and stretched his arm around me as best as his small body could manage. I knew then the song was done. After this, there would be no changes.

It went on to win the "Best Song" award in the *Nashville Scene* Critics Poll two years later, when it appeared on my *There, I Said It!* record. I play it every gig. People laugh and cry, and to think, I nearly threw that song off of the album when I was making it; I thought it was too honest. Who would want to hear me whine like that? But I put it on, and I may not have a swimming pool in an opulent back yard, but I've written a song that has apparently made a lot of parents feel like they're not alone. If nothing else, I've done that.

* * * * * *

Before there was ninth-grade Tina, there was seventh-grade Brenda Collins, the first female in my life who was poetically perfect. The first one to take my self-esteem to the gutter without having to do anything except just breathe and smile and toss her long brown hair.

It was church camp week, sleeping in cabins out in the woods with other almost-adolescents. Summer, 1975. I was 12.

This was the first year we in my age group might actually ask a date to the Friday night bonfire. We might be old enough to sing "Kumbaya" while holding hands with someone now, or maybe just sit next to each other and be wonderfully, newly together. That summer it went from something the big kids did to the greatest thing I could possibly do with my time on earth.

And suddenly, without Brenda, my life felt inferior now somehow.

As soon as I fell besotted over Brenda, my first following thought was . . .

"It's no use."

The matter was closed. There was no hope in my heart. Not a bit.

"It's no use."

Because I wanted her, I could not have her. I was not good enough. I just knew I wasn't somehow.

I never spoke to her. Not once. Some asshole named Skip took her to the bonfire. I sat next to them.

* * * * * *

It was Dad's birthday, a Sunday in December, after church. I think I was about 11. He was in his recliner, socks at 10 and 2, the playoffs on, snow clouds outside.

I was a little old to be cute anymore, but when you're the baby in the family you push it.

I found a cupcake and some birthday candles in the fridge and put one little blue candle in the center of the cupcake.

It was yellow cake with chocolate frosting in a little sky-blue corrugated paper cup, with a little blue candle burning in it.

I carried it gingerly into the living room.

I stood about five feet in front of my father, to the right of the television, knowing not to block it.

He cut his eyes over to me for what was honestly somewhere between one and two seconds, maybe three on the outside.

Then he cut his eyes back to the game.

I don't know how long I stood there. I don't remember if I actually hummed a little of "Happy Birthday" or if I just thought it, or if maybe it was somewhere in between and just died in my throat.

All I remember next is that little string of smoke rising off the candle, when it tipped over into the coffee grounds and the eggshells and the paper towels soaked in bacon grease, in the kitchen wastebasket. And with that hanging in the air like a spent match, let's move on.

feces raining from the sky

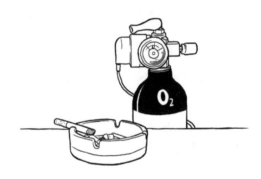

My full name is Tommy Glynn Womack. Not Thomas, Tommy. My middle brother, Jerry, had an imaginary playmate named Tommy and so when I came around, the word became flesh. I have no idea where the Glynn comes from. I never asked. You know what's funny, it's Glenn on my birth certificate. Is that Kentucky or what? My own birth certificate is misspelled. AC/CD.

I was born in Sturgis, Kentucky. The No. 1 song in the nation on November 20, 1962, was "Big Girls Don't Cry" by the Four Seasons. I came into a world full of four screaming Italians scratching their fingernails across a chalkboard in the sky. I bet they were playing on a radio in the delivery room when I was being born. Colored my whole life.

Kentucky-born I may have been, but I was Arkansan by blood and raising. It's not something you lean on for strength when life is hard. It's more something you soldier on in the face of.

Let's go back to the 1840s and the Homestead Act. In order to settle the new West, Uncle Sam declared a first-come/first-served policy for all the territory west of the Mississippi, to be given out in 40-acre allotments. If you got there first and staked your claim, that land was yours, in happy exchange for your being adventurous enough to pick up and go there. And it was stipulated that the race to the west would commence on such and such day of such and such month.

On that cold and early morning on the west side of the Mississippi River, thousands of families stretched out in a line for miles to the north and south. They were in Conestoga wagons, on buckboards; there were men on horseback and people walking, taking everything in the world they owned. There was a U.S. Marshal every mile or so, on horseback, about 30 yards in front of the pioneers, all straining against the leash. All the marshals up and down the land had synchronized their pocket watches via telegraph. They all held pistols aloft, and the moment the clock struck 7 a.m., the pistols fired. And off they all went! Great clouds of dust went heavenward as people lashed the backs of their horses and galloped at full tilt into the future. Some would make it as far as California, to strike it rich logging and fishing. Some made it to Nevada, and Colorado, and made their names as ranchers. Some made it to Kansas, Oklahoma, and Nebraska, becoming the breadbasket of the nation. Some went 17 miles, said fuck it, this'll do, and became Arkansas.

* * * * * *

Dad smoked all day long; he smoked like a man with issues. Two packs a day, easy.

If Dad could have gotten away with having an ashtray up at the pulpit, he would have done it. If he could have given the Benediction with a raised hand and a lit Camel fuming between upraised fingers, drifting smoke up to the cross behind him, he would have done it.

Papa Waters smoked like a man with issues too. He spent the last 15 years of his life gasping into an oxygen mask like a salmon on a dry riverbed.

By the time Dad died, he had the oxygen tank too, and he'd had so many organs removed one by one that if he'd lost any more, we would've had to mount his head on a heart-lung machine, and put him on the coffee table like a goddam science project. Better make me the science project. I haven't smoked a cig in two years, but my lungs are still a cesspool. And Dad and Papa Waters, they didn't drink whiskey, smoke pot, snort coke and pop pills like I have. I'm a walking experiment for the family tree. How ugly will my dotage be? I'm already on enough prescription drugs legal and otherwise to stun a horse.

Not that Arkansans have family trees. We have big picture frames with spots for eight different Kodak moments, in shapes from oval to heart to star to rectangle to this to that, and they hang on the wall next to the thermostat, next to the picture of Jesus, next to the couch, next to the oxygen tank and the elder person watching *Monday Night Football*.

* * * * * *

It's Saturday, May 15, 1994. I'm 31 years old with no hair loss yet, and I'm in Nashville onstage at 12th & Porter Playroom, bashing my well-worn Telecaster and playing with the bis-quits, with Will Kimbrough, Tommy Meyer, and the redoubtable Grimey, and we're shit-hot. It's sold out. You can't get another person in here with lubricant. And we're playing like demons. I mean, we are throwing it down, hard! We have a great CD on Oh, Boy! Records. Oh, hello there. What's that? We went to high school together? Oh, how cool! It's good to see you. What am I doing these days, you ask? I'M ON JOHN PRINE'S RECORD LABEL, MOTHERFUCKER!!

Back in high school I would listen to records in my bedroom. Loud. I would pretend I was the leader of the band, crank up the headphones and picture myself as the singer onstage. And now I am the singer on-stage. I'm INSIDE the stereo now. Will and I are bouncing guitar licks back and forth during the crazy rave-up lead break. We're playing "Yo Yo Ma," which has a Chuck Berry feel with a lot of NRBQ swing and a dollop of Replacements. The lead break builds and it builds, higher and higher, wilder and wilder, louder and louder, until we roar back into the chorus and the place goes bats.

This is all I've ever wanted. When I was in high school, I dreamed of being a rock star, a songwriter voice of a generation, and then people would applaud me and put my picture on their walls and write me neat letters and THAT would be my self-esteem! It doesn't work that way, and after nine years playing with two regionally beloved bands in quick succession, I know that now. But chasing the showbiz brass ring is just a habit now. It's how I think. It's become like Ahab and the Whale. Oh, fuck that right now. Let's rock 'n' roll all night. And party every day.

* * * * * *

Friday, November 25, 2011

My oldest brother, Waymond, died last month, eaten by cancer and grief. He lost his wife, Lou, in April, and was devastated. He and Lou liked a drink and a smoke, and it wasn't long after she died that Waymond was in a doctor's office being told he had cancer. What kind of cancer, nobody knows. He heard the doctor out, went home to his trailer and told no one what he knew. Five months later his stepson dropped by to find him in a wheelchair weighing 90 pounds, sucking oxygen from a tank WHILE SMOKING, drinking beer, eating nothing and existing past the point of no return. Waymond went to the hospital and never went home. He went like Papa Waters and Dad, slow and horrible. So tell me, Tommy, why do you drink? Why do you roll smoke? I say, Hey, sawbones, I'm just carrying on an old family tradition.

* * * * * *

How do you castrate a Hoosier? Kick his sister in the jaw. Two priests go into the jungle to convert the natives. A tribe captures them, takes them to the village and ties them to stakes. The tribal chieftain approaches the first priest and says, "Death . . . or boogaloo?!" The priest doesn't know what "boogaloo" is, but he doesn't want to die, so he chooses the unfamiliar option. The chieftain's eyes light up with joy, and he turns to the tribe and exclaims with delight, "Boogaloo!" Immediately, all the men of the tribe seize upon the priest, untie him, and then, as a group, they savagely rape him, repeatedly. It goes on for hours, the delirious tribesmen penetrating his every orifice while the priest cries in pain, horror and shame. At last they leave him bruised and naked in the dust, spattered with fluids and crying like a baby. The chieftain then approaches the second priest, still tied to the stake. "Death . . . or boogaloo?!" the chieftain demands. Having seen what his partner has just gone through, he says simply, "Death." Once again the chieftain's eyes go wild with delight, as he turns away to the tribe and joyfully shouts, "Death . . . by boogaloo!"

our father, who art in heaven, i'm really high

It is September 3, 1999, 3:10 a.m. EDT. I'm in Manhattan, and it has been an eventful night. I played a dinky opening slot as part of some college radio seminar, but I had a great band. Will Rigby from the dBs on drums, Mark Spencer from the Blood Oranges on guitar, fresh out of jail and drinking whiskey, and Scott Yoder on bass for a cozy 30-minute set at Under Acme.

Lonesome Bob and I came up from Nashville together in my GMC Jimmy. He did a set tonight. I did a set, then Amy Rigby, then Danielle Howle, then Johnny Dowd. It's been a cool night. Then what did I get to do? I got to go see the Dictators at CBGB. The almighty Dictators! If you'd told me when I was 15 that someday I'd see the Dictators at CBGB, I would have calmed down considerably. I did a gig in Nashville with Scott "Top Ten" Kempner and turned him on to Cheese Chronicles *and now I'm like buds with him and it's COOL. I am 37 years old, driving hither and yon playing rock 'n' roll, and I'm buds with Top Ten. And Adny! And Handsome Dick! Tonight I got to meet Ross the Boss for the first time. Oh, they rocked. Oh, it was great. The Dictators are tunes of my youth, man; I had all three albums! And Joey Ramone was there tonight. I said "howdy" and he said "hey" back to me. I am living the dream.*

I'm also currently in charge of steering a blue four-wheel-drive GMC Jimmy four-door in and amongst the anarchy that is Manhattan traffic. With a beery pot buzz. At 3:10 a.m. I'm supposed to be staying way up-town in the upper nineties, and I'm seeing signs for the Staten Island Ferry. So I turn around. No big deal. I've got Bob Dylan jamming in the cassette deck and he's singing one of my favorite lines: "Now you stand there expecting me to remember something you forgot to sayyyyyyy!"

Traffic clogs up as I nose my way back uptown into Soho. Eighty percent of the traffic is yellow. Those yellow cars are king wildebeests on the Serengeti. Traffic lanes mean nothing. A red light in New York City only means that if you were considering stopping, then this would be a good place to do it. It means nothing more than that. And here I am in a cluster of a dozen vehicles at a tricky light and I look over to the Cadillac next to me, and the cool Huggy Bear-looking dude driving it. "What are you looking at?" he appears to say to me as he glares. And then I notice the rising and lowering of a hairdo in the guy's lap! Oh! Sorry, man. I look away.

So I'm supposed to meet up with Lonesome Bob and crash with this fellow named John Something in the upper nineties. I have ascertained that the Lonesome One is at a certain bar in the mid-thirties, drinking with the Waco Brothers, which would mean serious drinking. I find the bar and there are the Wacos. Still pounding 'em. Those are rock 'n' rollers. "Oh, Bob? 'e pissed off about an hour ago."

So now I need a pay phone. (I do not have a cellphone yet at this time in my life.) And I need a New York City phone book, and I also need the slightest damn clue what could replace the name "Something" in the name "John Something." And then, God steps in. While fishing for quarters in my jeans pocket, I come across a little piece of paper. I unwad it to find written, "John Driscoll." Nothing else, just John Driscoll. Thank you, Jesus. I have one of those stoned-relief moments when your blood pressure has risen and then settles back down and suddenly you're so fucking happy.

Of course there have to be seven John Driscolls in the book, but only two in the nineties and gosh darn it if I don't score a goal with my first throw. "Hello? Hey, uh, this is Tommy Womack, Lonesome Bob's friend. Sorry to wake you. So, what's your address? Wait a sec, let me find something to write with. Okay, sorry, shoot. Great. Thanks, man. Yeah, see you in a few." I now have a proper address, written down on the same slip of paper, and life is fucking awesome.

I say my goodbyes to the Wacos and head back to my truck. When you've left your vehicle parked in New York City, it's always such a thrill to come back later and see it still there.

I suck down a roach in traffic, tossing the thumb-burning end out the driver's-side window. As I round the turn onto Central Park West for the charge uptown, I see one of Manhattan's pyramids of garbage bags to my right on the corner. After my turn I start to hear a FLAP FLAP FLAP and I figure I snagged a garbage bag. Only the FLAP FLAP FLAP sounds rather fat and large, and persists. At my first stoplight, I get out and run around the front of the truck real fast. Yep. Well, at least it's only flat on one side.

So what does one do with a flat tire at 72nd and Central Park West at getting close to four in the morning? You DRIVE ON IT, MUTHER-FUCKER! Twenty-three blocks uptown. All the way I'm hearing FLAP FLAP FLAP FLAP. I turn the Dylan off out of some buzzkill allergic reaction. I just drive my Jimmy uptown in New York City and listen to my right front tire, and possibly the wheel too, disintegrating.

But I make it. And I find John Driscoll's neck of the woods. Now to find a place to park. I narrow it down to a place near a pole with the least amount of complicated signage on it I can find. I hide all stealables as best I can, then shoulder my trusty Telecaster, my travel bag and my sleeping bag, and, so laden, I toddle off under my weight to find John Driscoll's digs in a nice New York brownstone. It is then I realize that, on the payphone earlier, I hadn't asked an important question. The apartment number.

(Real fast. With feeling.) "Our Father, who art in Heaven, hallowed be thy name. Thy kingdom come, thy will be done, on Earth as it is in Heaven. Give us this day our daily bread, and forgive us our trespasses, as we forgive those who trespass against us, even though I don't really get the word 'trespass' in this context. I suspect it meant something slightly different in Aramaic. ANYWAY. Lead us not into temptation, but deliver us from evil. For thine is the kingdom, the power, and, the glory, forever. In the name of the Father, the Son, and the Holy Ghost. Amen."

PRESS A BUTTON! ANY BUTTON! Cha-ching!!! WE HAVE A WINNER!

"Hi, I'm Tommy. Nice to meet you, John."

Fifteen minutes later I am laid out in my sleeping bag on the floor of John Driscoll's apartment, with Lonesome Bob snoring on the couch and naked girls on late-night Showtime. I'll deal with the flat tire tomorrow, and the possible permanent damage to the wheel as well. Right now I have titties on TV, and a latent post-trauma pot bliss. Rock 'n' roll. God has held me in his hands tonight. And someday I'll spend a lot of time thinking about what a snootful of shit I could have wound up with. But not tonight. Tonight is awesome. Good night, titties. Good night, Bob. Good night, Beth. Good night, John Boy. Good night, Nathan. Daddy misses you.

6

spleens, who needs 'em

Ever since I lost my spleen in '93, I've needed plenty of sleep. I don't know what the spleen has to do with sleep; I just know that's how I've been ever since.

I had a bike accident at age 31. Beth and I were bicycling around our neighborhood. When I tried to go from asphalt to sidewalk, the bike came out from under me. I flew over the handlebars, landing on my rib cage. My spleen ruptured and I commenced to bleed internally like Dottie West on a bad day.

Beth left me propped up against a sign, biked home to get the truck, came back and poured me into the passenger seat, slinging my bike into the back. I was leaning against the dashboard by the time we got to St. Thomas Hospital. Beth was a morning TV news anchor in those days. She asked a lady at a kiosk window where the ER was. "Oh my Lord, it's the Channel 5 lady!" "Yes, ma'am. Could you tell me where the emergency room is?" "You know you look even prettier in person!" "Thank you. My husband's dying, could you please tell me where to take him?"

For the next two weeks I was flat on my back with a major honking scar running down my belly and a garden hose up my willy.

You would be forgiven for thinking this was a bad time to be me, but it was wonderful. It's when I fell in love with Demerol. A month after I got out of the hospital I went on a 10-day tour with the bis-quits. I was not allowed to carry equipment and I was taken directly from the hotel to the gig, and directly back right after the gig. I was planed out on Darvon and thinking the whole time, "This must be what it feels like to be Keith Richards."

It would take me a long time to learn that painkillers don't like anybody. They act like they do, but it's a front. Painkillers make you want to drive two hours back and forth to your hometown to buy $60 worth of them. They want you to sit on the couch and listen to Rolling Stones bootlegs all day. They make you play way behind the beat. They make people not trust you. They make you think nobody can tell you're taking them. They make you think a prison is freedom.

* * * * * *

When I was 14 in 1977, I formed an imaginary band with three other classmates: Troy Howell, David Cates and Rufus Baker. We called the band Prostate.

We thought it an appropriately disgusting and provocative rock 'n' roll name, even though I doubt any of us knew what a prostate was yet.

I had an art-class assignment to design an album cover. On a stark black background, I glued on rather good penciled likenesses of the four of us, only with longer hair than we really had. Across the top was the name of the band, PROSTATE, in dripping letters of globular blood.

It was cool, it was disgusting, and it was provocative, like the Sex Pistols, whom we revered even though we'd never heard a lick of their music except on television. You couldn't get it in Kentucky where we lived.

That was 40 years ago. I've played rock 'n' roll for 30 years now, and I sure as hell know now what a prostate is.

I struggle with the dichotomy of banging my guitar onstage with youthful abandon while the commercials that run during the evening news resonate on my middle-aged ass.

Rock 'n' roll is sex, so is the blues, and so is country music (although you don't get oral sex in country). When I'm up onstage nowadays I figure I'd best be in tune and on-beat with lyrics that are a turn-on to listen to, because otherwise, so far as sex appeal goes, I'm up Shit Creek. There's nothing sexy about a 49-year-old man onstage, and everybody knows a doctor has stuck two gloved and lubed fingers up his ass to check out that prostate. And if you think that's disgusting, let's have lunch and you can watch me pick my nose like I left a goddam nickel up there.

＊＊＊＊＊＊

Tuesday, November 29, 2011

Well, I worked THREE hours today. That's better than yesterday. I swear I just haven't had it in me. You really have to psych yourself up to read these patient complaints, and you can't go more than 20 minutes before you have to get up and walk around for a minute, maybe look for something to gouge your eyes out with.

I'm supposed to meet with a guy tomorrow morning about writing movie scripts. He's a big fan of *Cheese Chronicles* and wants to meet at a Starbucks out in bumfuck. I don't know how good a screenwriter I could be but judging from what movies I've seen in the last couple of decades, I'd say the authors of these patient complaints could give the whole Hollywood guild a run for their money.

My Clash cover band, Tommy Gun, rehearses tomorrow night. That should be fun. It SHOULD be, but it's really just another thing on that long list of things that I would rather be sitting on the bed surfing the net instead of doing. So much of this shit used to be fun, but sometimes when I pick up my guitar now I just feel guilty that I'm not doing something else that could put bread on my family's table, 'cause I sure ain't doing it with this damn guitar. I love the guitar; I hate the damn thing.

＊＊＊＊＊＊

Thursday, December 1, 2011

For more than a few years now, I've been writing songs and playing gigs, but I can't just listen to music anymore. It competes with the voices in my head and the voices always win. They tell me all the time what a failure I am, and about all the fuckups I've strewn in my wake and the chemicals I've put in my body, and all the chances I've blown. If there's one person in the world who's ever not been screwed over by the record business, it's me. I've had every chance, and I've gotten stoned and blown it over and over again. And the voices tell me about that all the time. I'll drive five hours to a gig and not listen to a single song on the radio. It's an intrusion on my self-talk. I wonder how many other people go through the whole day with this same kind of noise in their heads. It gets exhausting.

Still, I write songs. I have to. Sometimes I sit down with my pad and paper and try to write one, and you can get some good stuff that way if you try hard; sometimes the song sneaks up behind you and says, Boo!

Write me! Back in the winter of 2005, I was at a bar in Franklin, Tennessee, listening to Bill and Dickie Brown's band play. I was sitting at the bar and a song, a big one, snuck up behind me and put me in a headlock.

I had no pen or paper, so I asked the bartender if he had any such things. He pulled a pen from behind his ear and gave it to me. But what about the paper? He didn't have any. Well, hey, could you spit me out some cash register ribbon? Giving me a quizzical side-glance, he hit the button on the register that spits out blank receipt paper, and he handed me about three inches' worth. I filled it up immediately and asked for more, he gave me more, and I filled that up too. I asked for more, and got him to give me a foot-long strip, and for over 20 minutes I asked for more paper, filled it up, asked for more, filled it up, and then the song was done, on 11 feet 4 inches of cash register ribbon, front and back.

Alpha Male and the Canine Mystery Blood

Alpha Male and the Canine Mystery Blood
came to town with Death Cab for Cutie
I stayed home with my wife and my child and a six-pack of beer
I pondered that name for fifteen minutes
after I saw the poster stapled to a phone pole on the corner of
    Grand and 21st
That was a couple of years ago, I was already in my forties then
so I didn't go out on a whim just to see a band called Alpha Male
    and the Canine Mystery Blood
just because I like the name, just as if I'm 25 and every day's a
    stoned summer day
My band was always gigging then, REM was still kicking then,
    I drove that Ford Granada Mom and Dad gave to me after
    they got 'em a Ford LTD, and there was music on MTV
I smoked my manager's pot and got laid quite a lot
Planes hadn't flown into towers yet and we didn't have a loose-
    cannon president
didn't have all this credit card debt hanging over the house like
    a cloud
insuring there's not a lot of drugging allowed
The body can't take it; the wallet won't hang
I'm singing all the songs I've sung for years, and when it's a band
    gig, it's rocking
and when it's solo, the people talking while I'm singing make me
    depressed
You think I could take a hint! My time came and went

Hell, there's many nights I came and went, in a manner of
      speaking
My conscience is leaking
The world has changed and the good times are gone
We get to be the folks who greet the dawn
of an age of mistrust, surveillance and sleaze
bombs in shoes and way too many enemies
I bet their name was Menstrual Blood and the A&R guy said
      "That's no good
You've go to change it to Mystery and then we can target a
      broader-based, Goth, dog-lover market"
I love my boy. He's becoming a drummer
He got a drum kit from Santa. At this rate by summer
he'll be keeping a beat in a world that needs a metronome shoved
      up its ass so hard
all voices will raise in a heavenly choir
shit'll get straight, brothers'll hug
we'll dance like we did in the decade of the good drugs
I'm spitting my genes in an ocean that's rising
clinging to Jesus with some compromising
of how it was handed to me from my mom and my daddy the
      preacher
who watched all that TV in a cream recliner
frowning through life like a stone hardliner
You couldn't faze him. He knew Jesus died for his sins and
      was raised from the dead. And I've always wondered,
      Why can't he stay dead?
It doesn't change any good thing he said
It was all St. Paul's trip, the Resurrection, why?
Why can't he be just a nice Jewish guy
who was super clued-in
and showed us the way to salvation from sin
And that doesn't mean if you're not quote-unquote "saved,"
you fry like a slice of country ham in your grave
It's a great big world. Life is a joke
Arabs & Christians. Pepsi & Coke
People so gorgeous, it causes 'em pain, and nobody gives any
      sympathy for something like that; you suffer in silence
or form a band
With a name that appeals to Goth dog-lovers everywhere
on a poster that's seen by a 40-ish bastard walking to work at 8:15
Eleven an hour for all that he does

Can't be a has-been when you never was
Going all day long without eating
'til all my nerve endings are seriously overheating
my legs getting wobbly walking down the stairs
to smoke me a cig in the cold fresh air
wondering why I do the things I do
And I do 'em every day
And it can't turn out good living this way!
But live my life I must, and in some fuzzy God I'll trust
I'll kiss my wife and I'll kiss my son
And maybe someday I'll go for a run!
Maybe someday a song'll stick!
I'll walk around like I got a big boat
Maybe someday my boy will drum
in a hippie jam band that plays out some.
He'll take after Daddy, get in a van,
go to places only young people can,
doing things only young people do,
banging those skins at Bonnaroo,
rocking the dreadheads dancing in the mud
before Alpha Male and the Canine Mystery Blood
God go with him
Amen

low-beating hearts and two david olneys for the price of one

The truth is a terrible thing. It colors everything it touches, and it paints a sell-by date on every lie you tell to other people and the ones you tell yourself. Those lies will rot in your gut and vex your spleen, if you still have one.

The lie is such a beautiful thing. It deflects everything in its path, it paints a great picture of yourself to people, but then you wonder why people over time start dismissing you as full of shit. And once you've been cold busted telling a whopper and somebody calls you on it, you're fucked with that person. Forever. They won't believe a word you say from then on.

Erring on the side of truth manifests itself as peace, more or less. Erring on the side of dishonesty reveals itself in mental fatigue from trying to keep your stories straight, and the stomach tightens. Respiration is affected. If you have any character at all, you feel guilt, and then one day a wise man from the east walks up and tells you, "The truth shall set you free, my child. Right after it pisses you off."

* * * * * * *

It's South by Southwest in Austin, Texas, March 2011. I'm in some dark, dingy club and I'm edging close to a painful memory that I'll have no clear recollection of.

I've got the shakes. I haven't eaten all day. I haven't had a drink in over six months. I've been patting myself on the back for that. And thank God I'm not shitfaced, considering everything else I've taken today: 40 milligrams of hydrocodone and an incredible number of Klonopin. I have no idea how many Klonopin I've taken. There looked like about 20 in the bottle when I got it this morning, and now they're almost all gone. I should be out like a light. Secretariat would be out like a light.

David Olney is playing his showcase before I play mine. I'm watching David play with Sergio Webb on guitar and Dan Seymour on bass. It's the wildest thing. David's playing and singing his heart out and six inches to his left is another David Olney, and he's playing the exact same thing as first one. Their lips are in perfect sync on every single word and their guitar playing is so tight it's like one person. That's when I know I'm going to suck tonight. If I'm watching a six-man trio 20 minutes from showtime, I'm going to suck. And there's not a thing in the world I can do about it.

Now it's my turn; I hug a couple of old friends on the way to the stage. They're so glad to see me. I won't see them after the show; they'll have left.

I strap on my guitar, step up to the mike, step away from the mike, take off my guitar and put it away in its case. That's how I'll remember it. Later, I'll be told what actually happened was I stepped up to the mike, played a 45-minute abortion and THEN stepped back and put away my guitar.

We drive back to the hotel, in two cars. Dan and I are in my car and, unbelievably, I'm fucking driving! Mary Sack, my manager (known as Sack), Sergio, and a friend of theirs are in the car behind us. Before we take off, I ask that friend in front of God and everybody for a hydrocodone, because I've heard he's holding. Amazingly, he gives me one. Sack hollers at me not to take it until we get back to the hotel. Whatever.

I'm in front because I have Emma, my GPS. "In point two miles . . . bear left." Or did she say bear right? Shit!

I zoom three lanes over to the right at the last possible second to miss taking the wrong fork, scaring the shit out of everybody in the following car, and probably Dan next to me, but he keeps his cool, he's had a few tokes. It was bad enough doing this once. So I do it twice, zipping over two other lanes. It's a damn good thing there are no other cars wherever I'm intending to go.

Next week I'll haul myself to a Narcotics Anonymous meeting for the first time in two years. I'll get the courage to walk up at the end of the meeting and pick up a white beginner key tag. I'll get a temporary sponsor. I'll do the whole bit like you're supposed to. Thus will begin another round of recovery meetings, with a lot of one step forward and eight steps back.

I'll also wind up damn lucky to still have a manager. Sack will be one of the people who will sternly insist the 45-minute abortion really happened. She was there, and she remembers it. That'll be more than I can say.

* * * * * *

My dad must have stopped digging at his toenails at some point, because in 1941, Mom gave birth to Carlton Waymond Womack, known by his middle name because that's how you do it in Arkansas. By now they lived in an apartment in Little Rock. Mom waited tables in a diner and Dad worked at a furniture factory. They were 18 and 23, respectively.

His work at the factory can't have been very physical. Dad was a very skinny man. (I inherited that.) He didn't have a lot of muscles and his idea of exercise was walking to the car. Once, many years later, I was 21 or so and trying on one of his old suits. He remarked, "Son, that suit would've fallen off me when I was your age." So here I was, skin and bones, and fatter than Dad was in 1941.

World War II was on but Dad was 4-F. The long-held family explanation for this has been that "his heart beat too low in his chest." This begs the question, what the fuck does that mean? I've never heard of a single instance where somebody's heart beat "too low in the chest." The army at that time was taking anybody who *had* a heart! I think they just didn't take his scrawny ass. "This one will die in boot camp. Next!"

* * * * * *

Q: How many ADD kids with Tourette's does it take to change a light bulb?

A: Let's go ride bikes, you cocksucker.

* * * * * *

Friday, December 2, 2011

Here was my day. I got up, took Nathan to school, came back home and tried to sleep some more because I was going to be up late at the Bluebird that night. A couple of hours later I showered and shaved, went to work for three hours trying to code those endless infernal complaints—*Waaah, my doctor wasn't nice enough, he kept me waiting! Boo fucking hoo!* Shut the fuck up!

I came home not long after Nathan got home from school, noticed that his new video game is rather gory, went back to my bedroom and watched crap television, then I went to a Kinks tribute band rehearsal over at Justin's house, sang until my throat was raw, then I went over to the Bluebird because I was on the guest list, caught the last bit of writers' round with Jim Lauderdale, Will Kimbrough, Eric Brace and Suzy Bogguss. I left during the last song because I didn't feel up to schmoozing. So I drove home, found Beth asleep and Nathan reading Harry Potter, I got him a Little Debbie cream cookie and a glass of water, went to my bedroom, hopped onto my spot in the bed and wrote this passage. These are my days, it's how I live. Good night.

* * * * * *

I've played rock 'n' roll professionally for 32 years now. I graduated Western Kentucky University in December 1984, with a B.A. in mass communication and a minor in writing. I long ago should have been sending out resumes and going on interviews. I did nothing of the sort. On New Year's Eve, I got a job at the Lee's Famous Recipe Fried Chicken on the 31W Bypass in Bowling Green, Kentucky, and I set about forming my first serious band, Government Cheese.

We stayed together seven years, we got on MTV, made a few dents in college radio, and played a mother load of gigs all over the place. We were terrible when we started but over time we honed into a damn good loosely tight rock 'n' roll combo. The slightly younger college kids in Bowling Green made us their local gods, and it happened in Louisville too, and Lexington, and Nashville and Knoxville, and a lot of other places. If you want the whole story of that band, go on Amazon and get yourself a copy of *Cheese Chronicles*. It's worth your time.

In '92, Beth got a job in Nashville as the Channel 5 morning anchor lady and the Cheese broke up at almost exactly the same time. I went south with Beth. And then, in Nashville, I found myself in the bis-quits, on John Prine's Oh Boy! label. That band broke up after two years because, when you're 29, playing for the door and sleeping on the floor is much less romantic than it was when you were 23.

I came out of those bands with nothing but a story, and I committed *Cheese Chronicles* to paper, the story of Government Cheese from top to bottom, pulling no punches and reasonably funny. A publisher in Nashville put it out. Suddenly, amongst a citywide population of aging rock 'n' rollers, I became "the guy that wrote that book," and it's become a cult classic if I say so myself.

I figured I was a writer now, and that's what I'd be for the rest of my life. I enjoyed it. And then, what happened . . . a producer friend wanted me to cut some of my songs in his studio. I said sure. That became my first solo album. And here I sit seven solo records later, 49 years old, no savings, playing solo acoustic gigs and working a day job, getting discouraged during the week when I'm home and then recharging my heart during every standing ovation I get at the end of the gig. House concerts are good for ovations, and sometimes clubs, but then sometimes the club is a bar full of frat guys and sorority Barbies and you wind up drinking a lot of vodka and wishing you had a flamethrower.

* * * * * *

More of Friday, December 2, 2011

My kingdom for a Xanax. I'm studying Kinks tunes for the tribute band I'm in. I'm heating up some soup so my stomach doesn't get too upset. At this point, I've run through all the songs, determined once again that without printed lyrics and chord sheets I'm well and truly fucked, and I'm wondering what of all this is any fun. I'm going to eat my soup now.

* * * * * *

Saturday, December 3, 2011

Wow. That rocked. Everybody loved it. And we made $90 apiece out of the hat-pass, which is a great night for the Family Wash. I sold a record and a book. So that's $30 more. I left a $100 bill on Beth's nightstand. We're going to do it again Friday, January 13. Maybe by then I'll have actually learned the songs, as opposed to reading chord changes off an internet transcription on a music stand that may not even be right to begin with.

It's 1 a.m. on a Saturday morning and where's my MSNBC *Lockup* marathon? Dammit. They're showing *To Catch a Predator*. I don't want that. I want convicts making pruno in their toilets and hiding shanks in their anal cavities. They really do that, you know. Can you imagine walking around on a prison exercise yard with a five-inch home-made knife up your ass? Ah, just checked the cable schedule. *Lockup: Wabash* comes on at 2. I'll still be up. I'm too jacked from the gig to sleep yet. Besides, Wabash is in Indiana, and there's nothing better than seeing Hoosiers in jail where they belong. I'm from Kentucky, remember. Us and Hoosiers, it's like Jews and Arabs.

I have to go to work later today. I'd rather drink dishwashing liquid. I have to go, though. Christmas is coming and it's taking no prisoners. Daddy needs bucks. I always know it's the season of giving when we get our Christmas card from South Nashville Heating & Cooling. Now to cram on a Tom Waits tune and two John Lennon songs for next Friday. Joy, joy. December in Nashville. The Tribute Gig Season. It gives us singer-songwriters something to do, as our type of acts have trouble booking gigs in the holiday season.

* * * * * *

I lived in Sturgis, Kentucky, for just a few short crawling and toddling years, late 1962 to early 1966, but I remember some things. The church Dad preached at was right next to our house, and there was a Tastee-Freez across the street. I remember that. That was my world.

I have four distinct memories, three of which I'll tell you right now. I remember Mom giving me a bath. I remember her holding me down on the floor with one arm while she tried to put drops in my eyes. And I remember sitting on the floor in front of the television watching the NBC Evening News with Huntley and Brinkley, and *knowing* it was Huntley and Brinkley.

One thing I don't remember at all is getting my leg broken. You'd think that would stick with a kid, but not me. My middle brother, Jerry, was sliding on his sock feet on the slick hardwood floor of the hallway. I could walk but not well, and I was apparently in his path. A collision was imminent. In the mayhem I got knocked over my older sister's doll bed and I fractured a bone in one of my legs. Which leg and which bone I can't tell you. A fresh snowfall had made driving dicey, and it is said that Dad carried me on his shoulders to the doctor, walking three blocks through the snow. I wound up in a cast up my leg for weeks. It's said I really learned how to walk with the cast on, adopting a bow-legged gait all around our house.

And this leads to my fourth and most vivid memory: the doctor taking off the cast. I remember this completely. Mom was at the end of the exam table, in the middle, wearing a green dress and a hat like you might see on *Leave It to Beaver,* Dad was beside her to the right, sporting his best skinny-tie, horn-rimmed Kennedy assassination look, and on the other side, to the left of Mom, was a white coated, wide-eyed maniac with a hacksaw attacking my leg. I remember that high-pitched sound of the saw and how this evil monster was going to saw my leg off for good and leave me to learn how to do without.

So there you have my four major Sturgis memories: taking a bath, being held down on the floor against my will, watching television and being attacked by a man with a saw.

8

90 miles an hour down a dead-end street

July 9, 2011

I went to Indy, in the rain
To a club that wasn't ever gonna have me again
A bottle of Chianti in the passenger seat
90 miles an hour down a dead-end street
I was lonely, lonely, I was tired
I work for myself and I still get fired
I came from Cleveland, with a gun
Six strings on it and I play every one
I love the Lord or at least I try
Where in the hell will I go when I die?
I like the Stones, I like dogs
I like late-night drunk dialogues
I went to Indy, in the rain
To a club that wasn't ever gonna have me again
A bottle of Chianti in the passenger seat
90 miles an hour down a dead-end street
I turn my foul-ups into rhyme
Life takes up a whole lot of my time

I still like booty on the street I see
But I'm not as horny as I used to be
And thank God for that! It's a pain in the ass
Waiting for the pangs of conscience to pass
Now I just drink, except when I don't
And you're either gonna get a good show or you won't
The highway's alive with a dangerous man
Acting as foolish as I possibly can
I drive on to Indy to play my show
Or maybe just play half a show and go
And drive on away with wine and weed
Thinkin' a spanking is what I need
I find me a hotel, get off the road
Get into bed, feel kinda cold
I didn't get busted, nobody died
I got me tomorrow to show a new side
Throw out the bad, keep all the good
Now I don't even know if I could
All of my blessings and all of my gifts
Teetering on the edge of a cliff
Drinking and driving all week long
Dancin' with the devil, looking for songs
I've done everything I can to kill myself and take other people
*   with me, by all rights I should be in prison, the Lord is my*
*   shepherd but LORD HOW I WANT!*
I went to Indy, in the rain
To a club that wasn't ever gonna have me again
A bottle of Chianti in the passenger seat
90 miles an hour down a dead-end street

* * * * * *

Somewhere in Little Rock, Arkansas, in the 1940s, Dad got the calling. Mom already had it. Grumpy cuss that he was notwithstanding, Dad was called to be a preacher, and Mom had the calling to be a preacher's wife.

It's not easy breaking into the preaching business, but like rock 'n' roll, anyone can try. You don't have to have any training certificate to be a preacher. A quick look at the religious cable channels will be enough to tell you that any moron with a passing knowledge of the Bible can get up and yammer.

I also think Dad wanted an audience. He had trouble relating tenderly to his wife and his young son; he needed the intimacy you only get from a roomful of strangers. There was no other line of work for nascent performers in Arkansas. Nobody was hiring actors, comedians or song-and-dance men, and Dad couldn't carry a tune in a bucket. Preaching was all there was.

* * * * * *

December 11, 2011

I get ulcers on my tongue, down my throat, on my lips, like Mom, and I suspect they come from not dealing with a lot of situations when they arose. Not responding to bullies and bitches seemed like the way to go back in high school. Turn the other cheek. Two wrongs don't make a right, Mom would say.

I have moments when my teeth lock up, my chest gets tight and my thoughts slow down until all I've got is the same angry image spinning around in my brain like an old stuck vinyl record. I'll find myself rehearsing a scenario in my head, like being in ninth grade and kneeling over Terrance, who used to call me a faggot, and I'm beating the shit out of him, my fists coming down into his teeth, my knuckles meeting his gums with delicious hard wet splats and my hands on the upswing slinging blood onto the ceiling above us while he cries like a baby. I could linger on that image for days. And have.

The problem though . . . I've kicked Terrance's ass in my head so many times he should be dead by now, but he's not. And that's the thing. His ass never really gets kicked. And the arguments I have with other people in my head, I never win them. It's just an image to savor, to gnaw on like it's a bone, with no resolution. And all it takes to table the whole matter is two tokes and I'm back listening to *Blood on the Tracks* and smiling while I channel-surf on mute.

Another problem, though. What you call munchies when you're 21 become sugar crashes from hell when you're middle-aged. I once got stuck in my Jimmy after having smoked half a joint before work and then finding I couldn't walk, having to call Beth on the cellphone to bring me some orange juice and a Hot Pocket.

* * * * * *

Everyone had roles in high school, and you didn't choose them; they chose you. I was the guy who was such a freak, so apparently out-to-lunch, so seemingly impossible to embarrass that he was almost cool. Almost.

I was a "Class B budding comic," which is a rare class clown mutation that occurs about 2 percent of the time, and is like that rare flower in England that stinks when it blooms.

Unlike the class clown, who actually gains acceptance among his or her peers via humor aimed at his audience, the budding comic is always onstage, always trying out new material, obnoxiously on a desperate search for humor, ALL THE TIME, just endlessly stringing the last two topics together and throwing them back out to see if it's funny, because laughter is love and love in high school is in short supply. Class clowns don't necessarily become comedians in later years. Almost all budding comics do.

* * * * * *

It is Thursday, February 22, 1979. I'm 16 years old and flat on my stupid face in love. I'm leaning against a locker like I'm cool. I'm blinking and chatting to Kacey Renfro while she rummages in her locker, distracted and running out of politeness. I took her to the homecoming this past weekend. For months I've thought she was cute, and when I plucked up the courage to ask her to the dance, and she actually said yes, my life went from black and white to color. I could hear birds. I could feel the sun. I felt cool. She said yes. I couldn't believe it. She said yes. We went to homecoming together. We sat together at the basketball game. We held hands. I went out with a girl. And now days later I am leaning against the locker next to hers, because I'm cool and I've been on a date with a girl. I'm cracking jokes because even love for you doesn't spare you my scattershot japery. I'm talking a mile a minute. It doesn't occur to me for a second that she just acted like she liked me long enough to have a date for homecoming. I keep talking and she's laughing sort of, and doing her best to be polite, but she reaches her breaking point, and she says "Tommy, just leave!" I am not the brightest bulb in the cabinet, but I do know that "Tommy, just leave!" is not something a girl says if she likes you. Maybe the reason she said, "Tommy, just leave!" is that she wants me to LEAVE. I'm leaning against the locker, because I'm cool, and it's one of those moments like at a urinal when you look down and see that you're peeing on your shirttail.

* * * * * *

December 24, 2011

Tomorrow we celebrate the birth of Jesus of Nazareth, who according to the Bible was born in the city of Bethlehem, the legendary hometown of King David, which is nowhere near Nazareth.

A Jew named Matthew wrote a gospel in the Bible. He wanted to persuade his fellow Jews that Jesus was the Messiah who had come to rescue the Jewish nation from its Roman occupiers and establish Israel once again as the great independent nation it had once been. That sounds more secular than what we consider a Messiah to be now, but in those days there was no separation between church and state. It was all the same thing.

Jews knew that the Messiah would be a descendant of King David, and would be born in David's hometown, Bethlehem. This had already been prophesied. So what Matthew did was write out a family tree—a bunch of hooey—connecting Jesus and David, and he came up with a moving and beautiful story that explained how Jesus was born in Bethlehem. He said that a young lady named Mary had conceived a child without any sort of sexual exploit (nice touch), and that her fiancé, Joseph, a descendant of David, went along with the program after an angel clued him in that the child would be the only Son of God, glossing over how an all-powerful deity could be held to a one-child policy, nor touching upon how this just made Jesus David's step-grandson at best.

Matthew wrote that the Roman ruler Augustus invoked a census and tax on every citizen of Israel, which would entail each adult male's having to go to his ancestral hometown to register and pay this tax. Joseph's hometown happened to be Bethlehem. Do you actually think you're going to stop *all business everywhere* so that *thousands* have to *go somewhere else* while carrying *money?* It's a highway bandit's dream. Nobody would have made it where they were going. And a pregnant woman on a donkey for miles and miles? Why not? It'll be fun.

Much as I enjoy debunking sacred texts, I also cherish the seasonal celebration of Mary, Joseph and their little baby Jesus, born in a barn in Bethlehem next to a 7-11 and laid in a feeding trough from whence he received a long line of gift-bearing well wishers. It is a sweet story, and it reminds me of my childhood.

I call myself a Fuzzy Buddhist Methodist, because I've gotten more comfort reading Buddhist teachings than I've ever gotten from the Bible. I grew up Cumberland Presbyterian, which is basically primitive Baptist with a change of necktie, but I'm Methodist now, which I like because Methodists can have wine with dinner. Now, as a Christian, I believe I possess a soul, but as a Buddhist I recognize that there's no such thing, and that's the "fuzzy" bit.

Nobody knows Jesus' real birthday. Second-century Christians in Rome settled on December 25 because it coincided with a Roman festival, and they could blend into the merriment and not stick out like a sore insurrectionist thumb.

Oh, fuck it, Merry Christmas, peace on Earth and goodwill toward men. Nothing wrong with any of that. I'll see you after Santa comes. And Santa's story is no bullshit. That fat fucker's real.

my night in a mental institution

July 2003

I Want a Cigarette

I was thinking I was the victim
Of some kind of family curse
So I went outside for a cigarette
So I could feel a little worse
And then I went back inside
Checked in with the nurse
Sat down in the waiting room
And scribbled down this verse

Life is complicated
It's wearing my ass out
Seems like I spend half my time
Wondering what the hell somebody's talking about
And they always think I'll understand them
Better if they shout
Sometimes I just don't believe
How much there is out there to doubt

Used to be so simple
When I was six years old
My butt would stay the color it was
As long as I did what I was told
And Daddy was a superman
With a big old hand for me to hold
Walking home from church at night
When the moon was bright and the air was cold

Sometimes I want to talk to God
And find out what I don't know
Sometimes I want to talk to God
And tell God where God can go
Sometimes I want kiss my woman
Hug her hard, love her slow
Sometimes I want a cigarette
A shot of booze and a rock 'n' roll show

The doctor said she'd see me now
And I could see her too
We sat in chairs and talked about
All the things we always do
It's this little game we play
She knew, I knew
A $30 co-pay later
I'd be leaving just as blue

Some folks go to parties
Other folks stay home
Some folks make a million dollars
In the time it takes me to find a comb
Some folks you can't trust 'em
Any further than you can throw 'em
Some folks you can grow up with
And one day find out you don't know 'em

But we all need something pretty
To hang onto at night
Some kind of faith that after dark
The morning brings the morning light
The world will do some more turning
Stars'll come out shining bright

Right now I want a cigarette
And maybe then I'll feel alright

* * * * * *

I really did write the first verse of that song in the doctor's office, but none of the other verses were committed to paper at all. My lunch break at Vanderbilt was a can of Diet Coke and five cigarettes, with me in back of the building out of sight. I would think of a line, settle on one, think of the next line, rehearse it in my head a little, think of the next line and so on, memorizing as I went. I've always been able to remember songs with a lot of words in them, even as I was writing them. "Betty Was Black"—wrote it cleaning the apartment in 1989, never wrote a word down. "For the Battered," either.

* * * * * *

I can gripe about shit gigs and near-poverty and substance abuse and working for the man. But it sure as hell isn't 2003 when I was 40. Nothing's as bad as 2003 was.

That's the year the marijuana turned on me, when I had a nervous breakdown and had to cancel a bunch of gigs because I couldn't stop crying long enough to do anything.

One hot July day in 2003, I went to see my counselor about three in the afternoon. I was an hour early, I had nowhere else to go and nothing to do but sit in her waiting room enjoying the air-conditioning, reading *Entertainment Weekly* and listening to Oldies 96.3 softly playing "Mrs. Brown, You've Got a Lovely Daughter."

It was a weekly thing, our visits. She was a nice lady. We had a routine—I came into her office, sat down in a comfy chair, whined, she took notes, gave me feedback, and so we did the counseling dance. I'd been seeing her for almost a year at that point and she was one more in the long line of counselors or shrinks or social workers that I've been seeing since 1979.

I was feeling particularly bad that Tuesday. I'd been at my Vandy job at the time—a temp job where I more hung out than worked. (This was years before I worked in patient complaints.) I'd had a lump in my throat like a big chunk of steak that wouldn't go down; I also had a sore throat and a headache, which happened when I was really depressed. On top of that I was starvation-level hungry. People don't understand why you don't eat when you're depressed. I don't understand it, either.

You just don't eat sometimes. Why prolong life and continue this misery, I reckon.

Oh, yeah, the counselor. So I had an appointment with the counselor at 4 p.m.

I left Vandy and walked the four or five blocks off campus to where I can park for free, got into my van and drove over to my counselor's office having no idea I wouldn't be driving away very soon.

She could tell I was in a bad way. The last time I was this depressed had been six weeks before, and she'd recommended hospitalization then, but my son's birthday was that next weekend and I had a couple of Todd Snider gigs I was opening at and didn't want to miss. Now I had no such gigs coming up. She asked if I felt I needed to be hospitalized and I said that it wasn't for me to say. You're the professional, you tell me. She felt it was the thing to do. Before I knew it we were walking over to Parthenon Pavilion (the primo mental hospital in Nashville), right across the parking lot, which is where I'd be hospitalized.

I was warming to the idea. I was thinking of the kind of hospital like any I'd been in before—television in the room, phone in the room, Beth could bring me magazines, maybe they'd give me some Valium and I could get a nice vacation from the world for a while. Maybe it'd be a nice thing.

But despite that rosy scenario, as I filled out some forms in a little room, the tears really started to come. "I can't believe this is happening," I remember saying. My counselor was gone, back to her appointments with other fucked-up people. A nice fellow from Parthenon named Ken had replaced her in my life and he started asking me a lot of questions.

Do you feel like you're a danger to yourself? Do you feel like you're a danger to others? Do you keep firearms in your home? I thought about breaking into "Skinny & Small" for him, a murder ballad of mine. I sat on the idea.

It occurred to me that this was all going to come as a surprise to Beth. And five-year-old Nathan, an impossibly cute kid, would miss his daddy tonight. Ken kept asking me questions and brought me forms to sign. Then he said I was prepped and my room was ready. I was now in a mental hospital. I'd finally fulfilled the prognostications of so many people.

Ken led me down a hall where he had to unlock a couple of doors that automatically locked again behind us with a loud *ka-chunkety-click*. Then he had to unlock the elevator with a key. Then we were on the third floor, walked across the hallway and he unlocked another door. We went inside. And that's when I saw this was no hospital with a television and phone in every room. You know *One Flew Over the Cuckoo's Nest*? This was it.

The place was flooded with fluorescent light. The ceiling was half Masonite, half fluorescent light. The floor was white linoleum. The walls were shiny cinderblock. The whole room was really bright. There was one television against the wall across this great room, with a bunch of chairs in a three-sided rectangle boxing it in, a coffee table with magazines in the middle. There was an old lady with long stringy hair sitting at a table working a puzzle. There was an emaciated middle-aged woman sitting in a chair and shaking uncontrollably. There was a big man in a hospital gown shuffling around, and a dazed-looking young woman in a wheelchair. There was a pool table, and a bookshelf, and three or four other people lounging around and chatting and looking cheerful and everybody had white medical wristbands on, including me. And in the corner, next to the door I'd just come in, was the win-dowed nurses' area, just like Nurse Ratched's place. This was it. This was the hospital.

Next thing I knew I was sitting in a chair answering more questions from a nice nurse named Leah, while I watched snot fall on my pants and tears make little gray circles on my shirt, thinking holy fucking shit, Tommy, what have you gotten yourself into this time? They took my cellphone, they took my cigarettes, and they took my wallet, took out all the important stuff (driver's license, credit cards) and gave me the wallet back. Since I'd mentioned suicidal thoughts before to my coun-selor and she had squealed on me, they also took the laces out of my shoes and took my belt from me too. My pants began hanging down to my hip bones and my shoes were loose wraps around my feet. So now I was busting a sag and was going to have to slide my feet everywhere to keep from coming out of my shoes.

All the bedrooms came off the main room where the television and the pool table were, and where the old lady was still working on her puzzle. There was a fellow named Mac who took me by the arm and escorted me to my room along with a nurse, not Leah, some other nurse. It was time for the strip search. Mac told me to step into the bathroom. I noticed a faint odor of a pair of underwear with skid marks in them.

"Take your pants and shirt off," Mac said. So I did. "Now drop your drawers." I wanted to say, "Are you serious?" but I just did what he told me to do. This is when I noticed that he had a latex glove on one hand. "Now turn around."

(I did.) "Spread your cheeks." (I did.) "That's fine." He concluded in a nicer voice. My anus must have looked like one that doesn't get shanks shoved inside of it.

"Can I put my clothes back on now?" I sniffled. "Sure," he said. So I did, quickly, as the crying shifting into high gear again.

"What's the matter?" Mac asked with a glassy smile, as if, now that he'd seen my anus, we were friends somehow. I think I said something like, This is all such a shock, or something, I don't remember. I must have said something about being depressed, because he put his hand on my shoulder and asked me my name. "Tommy," I sniffed.

"Well, Tommy," Mac said, "I suffer from depression too. I'm also a recovering alcoholic and drug addict. And you know ..." he pointed to the window in my room, "there's hope out there. There's HOPE!" Mac wore a necklace with key tags hanging from it. Narcotics Anonymous. NA is to AA what Fugazi is to Bon Jovi. An NA member with a year of recovery will have as many as a dozen key tags on a necklace, as he walks like a tinkly Buddhist bell, wordlessly chanting, "I will not smoke crack today, I will not smoke crack today."

"There's hope out there," he repeated, looking at me with a smile like a television preacher's. I noticed the "out there" part. He didn't say "in HERE," he said "out THERE." I heard Vincent Price in my head saying, "Abandon all hope ye who enter here."

Soon it was time for "patio break." I was lucky. If I'd missed this one it would have been two more hours, and I had never needed a cigarette in my life like I needed one right then. All we smokers gathered up front next to the Nurse Ratched window and got two of our cigarettes each (not our lighter); then a nurse unlocked the front door of the ward and led us across the hall.

We were led out into the hallway to the elevator, which was also locked. The nurse took her key and unlocked it. We stepped inside. The door swung shut. We traveled downstairs, the door opened, and we were led down a hallway to another door, which also had to be unlocked, and we stepped inside a hallway. The door shut behind us and relocked itself. At the end of that corridor was another door, which, yes, the nurse unlocked, and then we were on the patio.

The nurse gave one patient the lighter and we all gathered around it. Once we'd all gotten a cigarette going, the nurse took the lighter back. There was a semicircle of benches. On three sides the building rose up with all the windows of all the different rooms. On one side was a wall, a sheer wall, a very tall and sheer slate stone wall. Above us all was the sky. The clouds moved across the blue and we all looked up at it instinctively.

I was weeping slightly, sitting on a bench next to a nice, well-dressed fellow named Duane. He had a smile with great teeth, white like a Formica countertop, straight and even like little white soldiers.

"What's your name?" he smiled and asked. "Tommy," I sniffed, blowing out smoke. "Sorry," I added, "I'm a little overcome." "You depressed?" he smiled.

"Oh, yeah," I said. "So am I!" he added brightly. "I'm suicidal!" It was like he was saying, "I'm a third-degree Mason!" or something. "I'm also bulimic!" he added brightly. I noticed he had laces in his shoes. He's happily suicidal and keeps his laces. This place is corrupt.

"Oh, I've got a lot of problems," he said, with a mouthful of teeth that don't occur in nature. "Tomorrow's my birthday! How's that for depressing?" he said, laughing a little. "How old will you be?" I asked. "Thirty-one," he replied. "How old are you?" "Forty," I said, lighting my second cigarette on the ash of the first one.

Then we were led back up through the gauntlet of locked doors, back to the ward. Some horrible ABC sitcom was on the television, I think a Jim Belushi one, I'm not sure. One of the happy ladies asked if anyone was watching it. And since no one objected, she moved it over to NBC. *Fear Factor*, I think it was. This appeared to please her greatly.

Her name was Rita. She and another lady and two fellows were the ones who looked happy to be here. And Duane, of course. A very fat woman in pajamas was sitting there, along with the dazed-looking woman I'd seen before. The old lady was still working the puzzle; the emaciated woman was still sitting in her seat, trembling. There was another lady sitting alone to the left of the television. She looked, if anything, sadder than any of us. There were a couple of beet-red gash marks on her neck.

I went over to the bookshelf. There was one romance novel and about 20 old ratty *Readers' Digest* Condensed Books. My parents always used to get those. I looked for one I might recognize. I didn't want to read anything new; I wanted one I'd seen before. I wanted some familiarity. I didn't find any.

I said "Excuse me" very softly as I moved in front of the television and looked at the magazines on the low table there at the center of all the chairs. *Family Circle* was one of them (didn't want to see any pictures of kids because it would remind me of my own I couldn't see) and for some reason *Kiplinger's Financial Report*. Now who in the hell would be reading *Kiplinger's Financial Report* in here? I thought.

Oh, yeah, I remembered, the magazines come from doctors. Doctors want to read that shit. The front cover had some white guy in an Izod shirt laughing on a sailboat with his white wife. And they were so happy because their 401K is on steroids, the Republicans are in control and they're not locked in a mental ward without their belts and shoelaces.

So I went to my room. I decided to investigate what was in there. Talk about barren. There was nothing on the walls, no Ray Harm bird prints, no Ansel Adams mountains, no Monet, nothing but cinderblock. I guess that was because if you had art on the walls, some crazy person could pull it off and smash it. There were two beds, one of them mine, one of them, mercifully, nobody's. There was a bureau drawer that stretched across the opposite wall. There were two windows with the blinds pulled shut. There was the small bathroom where I'd had the lovely strip search earlier, and now I noticed that the mirror inside was polished aluminum, not glass. I noticed the faint skid-marked underwear smell again.

I sat on my bed and regarded the little three-drawer wooden nightstand next to it. I did what I always do in every hotel room. You know there's nothing in the drawers, but you look anyway. Maybe this time there'd be a Gideon Bible or something. I opened the top drawer. Nothing. I opened the second drawer and whoosh, the smell! Someone at one time or another had shit in that drawer. The shit was gone but the smell was there. Some crazy fucker shit in that drawer! That's fucked up. So I lay back on the bed and thought of Martin Luther.

That's not the stretch you might think it is, from feces to the leader of the Protestant Reformation. At one point in his life, Martin Luther used to sling his own feces at visions of Satan. He was under a strain at the time. The Catholic Church in the 1400s was appallingly corrupt, and Martin had done something about it. He had a church in Germany and one day he nailed his 95 Theses to the church door. I haven't read them but I know they boil down to "Yo! Yo! This is bullshit!" The pope sent "emissaries" from Rome to Germany to kill Martin or put him on trial, depending on how they felt when they got there.

Some friendly monks hid him out in the Black Forest, in basically a safe house, and that's where the stress of being the most wanted man in Europe got to him. The other monks took Martin's clothes away so he couldn't hurt himself and locked him in a cell for his own protection, where he began to have visions of Satan in the room with him. Having no other weapon, Martin Luther took to slinging his own feces at Satan, spattering the walls with his own shit. And now there are millions of Lutherans. I wondered how often they mention this in their church services, or do they just gloss over the whole incident? I wondered if there is a Lutheran Flying Turd Blessing.

St. Martin, we thank thee
for thou hast flung
thine own shitte

at our oppressor
so that we,
by thy grace,
might toucheth not our shitte,
nor fling it,
nor smear it on the sheep
or the antelope,
but instead,
by thy righteousness,
we may flush our own shitte
and toucheth not the turde.
Amen

There were two phones, 10-minute time limit. I called Beth again. I'd called her three or four times already. I think this time on the phone I just said "Oh God, oh God, oh God" over and over again.

Then it was time for Goals Group. This was my first meeting. All the patients gathered in the seats around the television. The nurse called the meeting to order. Everyone started the day with a goal, and now it was time to see if the goals had been met. One person said her goal was to have a tear-free day and she'd accomplished that (praise all around). Another lady (the slack-jawed one) said her goal was to remember everybody's names. She couldn't do it. The big fellow, Jerome, had the same goal, and he couldn't do it, either.

It came to my attention that they were both ECT patients—electro-convulsive therapy. That's what happens when nothing else works. When you've been through Prozac, Zoloft, Effexor, Paxil, Shadrach, Meshach and Abednigo and nothing makes you feel better. That's when they put a stick in your mouth so you don't swallow your tongue, wrap metal bands around your head, and juice you with enough voltage to reheat leftovers. This has actually been shown to bring hopelessly depressed people out of their torpor long enough to at least have a conversation. I didn't meet the slack-jawed lady nor Jerome prior to their being shocked, so I don't know firsthand how effective it is, but I can tell you it makes it really hard to remember people's names.

Goals Group went around the room and then it was time for me to introduce myself. I was crying my ass off again, but I got a few words out.

"My name's Tommy," sniff, heave, bawl, "I'm sorry, folks. I'm in here because," waah, sniff, "I-I get depressed and I'm sorry, this is all a bit of a shock, I-I didn't expect to, I thought I'd be home for dinner tonight, I WANNA SEE MY BOY!" I couldn't say any more.

And this is where I've got to hand it to these people. They were nice to me. Jerome patted me on the shoulder. Another lady brought me a roll of tissue paper. A couple of other people patted me on the shoulder, too. I was grateful for that.

"Well, Tommy," the nurse holding the meeting said, "it sounds like you're right in the place where you need to be." I didn't reply to that. Agreeing with her would have sounded like pandering and telling her to go fuck herself didn't seem like the right thing to say, either. So I said nothing.

Then it was medication time. The nurses brought out trays with little plastic shot glasses labeled for each of us. Some people had one or two little pills; some people had multicolored piles of medicines almost spilling out of the little containers. I had one little pill, something called Sonata. It was to help me sleep. Thank God for that, I thought, and washed the little thing down with some water, hoping the effect was immediate, and I'd pass out right there on the floor. It wasn't immediate, but it was time for another patio break anyway. Again we were lined up and given two cigarettes each and led through all the locked doors downstairs.

The first time I'd been too dazed at my loss of liberty. This time I was furious. How DARE you tell me when to smoke and how much I can smoke and where I can do it! This is America! This time on the patio, Duane wasn't as happy. "It's dark," he said. "I don't like it when it gets dark." We sat smoking and the conversation in our little group centered on our fathers. It appeared that none of us had fathers who gave us enough love. Confessions were made, tears were shed, cigs were lit on the ends of the first ones, and we were led back upstairs again.

I thought I felt the Sonata working, so I went to bed immediately. It was 9:30. Over the next two hours I figured out that Sonata doesn't do jack shit. I lay there and lay there. And then I lay there some more. And I prayed. Oh, boy, did I pray. I interlaced my fingers and prayed like a POW, like Martin Luther with shit on his hands, like a 15-year-old girl on the pioneer plains giving breech birth in a thunderstorm.

Jesus, please, if you're there
and I go back and forth on that
please come to me
give me some kind of sign
some sense I'm not alone,
a mouse doing the moonwalk,
anything!
Amen

I prayed like this because I have a friend named Bill and Jesus actually DID come to him when he needed it most. Bill is the same Bill as was onstage when I wrote "Alpha Male & the Canine Mystery Blood." He used to drink and drive. A lot.

So Bill was lying in the drunk tank one night and he knew he was fucked. This was his third DUI and he was going to jail. He knew it. He was looking at losing his job, maybe his family, his house, maybe everything. There was a door off to the side of the drunk tank and it was locked, but some light was coming through the bottom of it, and he heard someone on the other side of the door. As Bill lay there, bemoaning his fate, a voice on the other side of the door said, "You'll be alright. You just need to quit drinkin'."

The next day, as he was being released on bond, Bill asked to speak to the man on the other side of the door. What man, he was asked, and for that matter, what door? Well, the door in question turned out to be a utility closet, with brooms, mops, a bucket and no light bulb. Bill's been a clean-and-sober churchgoer ever since.

I do believe God answers all prayers and he answered mine. The answer was fuck you.

> *You're in an air-conditioned building*
> *and you're asking me for something?*
> *I've got thousands of people homeless in Nashville*
> *and you're in a room with clean sheets*
> *and you're asking me for something?*
> *You have free will;*
> *get your OWN shit together.*
> *I love you, Tommy, I really do,*
> *but Jesus Christ, man!*

Something obnoxious happens over and over all night: You close your door so no more of the fluorescent light is coming in, then the nurses do rounds, check on you, and then leave the door open! I got up four times and closed the door again and after the fourth time, I was up for good.

I stepped outside into the main room. And I overdosed. It wasn't drugs. It wasn't the imprisonment. It was the goddam fluorescent light! It had bothered me earlier, for sure. But now, with the sleep deprivation and my emotions like a top E-string tuned up to G-sharp—it got to me. If there's one thing I hate more than the Dave Matthews Band, it's goddam fluorescent light. It flickers, it blinds, it gives me a headache. I even wore blue-tinted glasses, I hated it so much. And now, at 3:30 a.m., with every other light in the ceiling turned off, it was still blinding.

There was one nurse up front, dozing in a chair. She stirred as I approached her. "Hi!" she smiled. I was choked up again. "Is there," sniff, "anything to EAT around here?" "Why, yes!" she said, "Look back there in the kitchen." She pointed back to a room next to where the phones were. "There's ice cream and apples and bananas and all sorts of stuff." I found a cup of chocolate ice cream and went looking for a plastic spoon in a big bag of utensils. All I found were forks. I scattered the forks all over a table in a search for a spoon. I never found one. I stabbed the ice cream with a plastic fork and broke one of the tines loose. So I put the cup of ice cream in my room to let it soften up. I went out to the big room again, to see if any of the magazines had mated and given birth to another *Newsweek,* or a *Mojo* or something. There wasn't any such Immaculate Periodical Conception, so I went back to my room and read the *Newsweek* all over again, eating the ice cream with my three-tined plastic fork as it melted.

Next thing I knew I was up front talking to the nurse again. I don't remember walking back up to her. I just remember sitting in a chair across from her and crying my eyes out. And I remember how she talked to me. Like I was a batshit lunatic who belonged in here.

There is a policy in mental wards. The patient is to be considered crazy until proven otherwise. That's how all the nurses talked to us. And it works in a contrary way. It *drives* you crazy if you're not there already. I'm not crazy, I felt; I don't care what Todd Snider says. I'm just depressed. And panicking. And crying. And when you're sitting in a chair in a backless gown with a white wristband on and you look a fright from crying most of the last ten hours, you've got a long-ass way to proving you're not crazy like the nurses think you are to begin with.

So she talked to me, very slowly. "Callllllm dowwnnnnnnnn, re-laxxxxxxx, take deeeeeeep breathsssss . . ." The more she tried to calm me down, the harder I cried. I was starting to hyperventilate.

She gave me a Klonopin. Then she went back to her mantras—"Callllllm dowwnnnnnnnn, re-laxxxxxxx, take deeeeeeep breathsssss . . . give the medication tiiiiiiiiiiime to wooooorrrrrrkkkk . . ."

And finally, at 5 a.m., the Klonopin kicked in. Poor man's Xanax or not, when Klonopin kicks in, you've got a nice 10-hour sleep coming up. Maybe 12. Sometimes, 14, 16—unless you're in a mental ward.

"GOOD MORNING, IT'S SEVEN O'CLOCK, TIME TO GET UP, BREAKFAST IS AT EIGHT!" With the Klonopin seeped into every bone and nerve in my body, I lurched up and got dressed. Then I fell back on the bed. Next thing I knew it was 8 a.m. and I was standing up, in the main room, in a line with all the cattle, and we went through all the locked doors and down to the cafeteria.

We all had to eat together at the same table, and we all had to stay seated until it was time to go back. I ate some eggs and bacon and hash browns and a jelly donut, and sat with my eyes closed in a Klonopin fog, and then we were back up in the ward again.

Goals Group. What's your goal, Tommy? I don't have one. Oh, come on, think of one. Okay, I want to talk to my boy. Oh, that's a good one.

My doctor came on rounds around 10. I begged him to let me go. "You know," he began, "that's not an unusual feeling for the first day here, but many people get over it and oftentimes by the end of their treatment they don't want to leave." I was having none of that, and over the course of about five more minutes haggling with him, he agreed to start the paperwork.

But paperwork takes a while. I was still there in time for the first patio break. Smoking down under the sunlit sky, Jerome asked me, "You leavin' us?"

"Yep."

"Don't like us?"

"Don't like locked doors."

A little over an hour later, when all the paperwork was done, the nurse unlocked the front door of the ward. I followed her, with laces in my shoes, a belt around my waist and my cellphone happily dangling on my hip.

She unlocked the elevator, and we went downstairs. She unlocked a couple more doors. And there was the lobby. I had to wait for one more piece of paper to be signed. It was like being a thoroughbred at the gate.

With the last signed piece of paper in my hand, I went for the first of two sliding lobby doors. The first one slid open and I walked through the breezeway so fast that the second one had hardly time to open and I missed hitting it by about an inch. I was on the sidewalk. And free.

I ran back to my van, called Beth from behind the wheel, bought a pack of cigs and a Diet Coke, drove home and hugged my wife and little boy. And that was it. And you know what? I regard it now as a rather positive experience. I sure wasn't as depressed coming out as I was going in, for one thing. I never had known what getting my personal liberty taken away felt like. Now I knew.

There were a few people in there who didn't want to leave. They didn't WANT to see their family members any time soon. I understand. Some families are like that. But I couldn't wait to see mine. The thought of being locked in somewhere was bad enough, but locked in without being able to see my son at all was intolerable. I've never been happier to see them than I was when I got home. And I thought that maybe now I'd feel better occasionally, just walking down the street. Because I'd have a little more insight on what it's like not to be able to walk down the street. Not to be trusted with your own shoelaces and not be fully human for a while. A pinch of that shit goes a long damn way.

At this point, I figured I'd never beat the depression. Abraham Lincoln never got over his. Winston Churchill had it so bad he stayed tanked for two World Wars. My pills weren't helping. My therapy wasn't helping. All that was left would be to hook me up to the ECT machine and juice me 'til I'm ash.

welcome, sir, this is the big time

In September of 2003, a month into a new temp placement in Vanderbilt's political science department and five weeks since my night of paradise in the laughing academy, I got an email from Todd Snider asking me to play bass for him. He was reforming his old band, Todd Snider and the Nervous Wrecks, for a one-off gig: two nights in a casino in Sparks, Nevada, next to Reno. Their old bassist had found God and so they needed a new one.

I had never played bass professionally in my life and from what I could gather the only reason Todd asked me is that he liked me and wanted me in the band. I crafted an email to Professor Tate, the department chair and my boss, half-cajoling and half-begging him to let me take time off to fly to Nevada and play the gigs. He assented. He actually turned out to be a big fan of the type of Americana songs I was associated with, and would turn out to be very supportive of me in that pursuit.

I had two weeks and no bass. I didn't own one. I found one to borrow. Quite a beauty, actually. A Fender Precision from the fifties that Robin Eaton had. It should have been in a museum. Somebody working for Todd sent me a CD in the mail of 25 songs. I sat in the bedroom night after night drinking wine and playing along with that CD on a boom box. It was good for me. Remember, no time was worse than 2003 and the crying spells.

By this point in life I'd had four solo records that went nowhere, I was torpedoed by drugs and drinking, my antidepressants weren't working what with all the other soporifics I was loading up my bloodstream with, I was washed up and plopped by circumstance into a dead-end job that would have been a nightmare even without a hostile supervisor and the tension and bad juju that was bubbling closer to the surface every day I had to go into that godforsaken office.

I worked my ass off with that CD and that bass. I didn't chart the songs out; I learned them by heart. Five hours a night after work Beth and Nathan left me alone as I devoted myself to going from a guy who'd never been a pro bass player in his life to being the new Bill Wyman. My right thumb grew a huge blister that burst and I played through the pain as the skin grew callused and assumed the texture of rawhide. Bass playing is the least understood role of all of the parts that make up a group. It's a Zen study in how little you can play and still get your point across. Nine times out of ten, you don't want the listener to notice you're even there. It's not a lead instrument (John Entwistle and Jack Bruce notwithstanding). The guitarist and the piano player get to do all the flash; the bass player is just there to play dark low notes and make everything sound full. That doesn't mean you can't do cool phrases here and there and jazz things up, but it does mean that if you're a bass newbie *and* a basket case, you might consider playing it straight.

The preeminent aspect of bass playing—and the deepest Zen of it—is that you become one with the drummer, especially with the bass drum and the snare. All your notes have to fall exactly in line with those drumbeats, neither a microsecond before nor a microsecond after, but exactly with the beating of the drum. The drummer is the boss. He's not going to follow you. He's a guy who bangs on things for a living. He can barely hear you. You have to surrender your ego and your self-will and synchronize your own literal heartbeat to his. Whenever he hits his bass drum, that's when you hit a note on your bass guitar, and you do it so cleanly and accurately that the result is that no one even notices you're onstage. You make the band sound huge but you disappear into the background at the same time. It was an ideal role for me at that time. If you want to feel "centered," you can't do much better than playing bass in a rock band.

Todd Snider is about one-quarter Jerry Jeff Walker, one-quarter John Prine and fifty percent his own original stoner dude self. (Throw a little Mitch Hedberg in there.) He's funny as hell and writes songs that are sidesplitting one moment and heartbreaking the next. He may be the most naturally talented person I've ever known, and it was all the more amazing given how stoned he almost always was. I've been asked whether the stoned, wine-drunk act was for real. He's not so far gone these days, but when I was with him it was absolutely true. He'd be out of his skull up there in the spotlight. But he was also weirdly professional. As baked as he was, Todd never walked onstage without a set list, and he never opened his mouth without knowing exactly what he was going to say. He told long, hilarious stories between songs, and he would never trip up. Perhaps he could do what he does sober. I don't know. But I stood to his rear left onstage and fully took in what a master looks and sounds like when he's in his element and higher than the Space Shuttle.

I found myself in a position I've grown all too familiar with: the one hack musician with a straight job in a band full of big dogs who piss in tall grass. Will Kimbrough was on guitar, Paul Buchignani on drums and David Zollo on piano. Heavy hitters. There was no rehearsal, save a lengthy sound check. This is how heavy hitters from Nashville do it. They don't like to rehearse. They'd rather go out there cold and burn it up. I'm not that way at all, and I wound up on that stage terrified.

There is a crucial aspect of bass playing that I became aware of only when doing the show itself. The bass player is the one guy in the band who has to know *exactly how the song goes.* I mean exactly! No room for mistakes. The guitarist and piano player can lay out for a split second and see where they are, all the drummer really needs to know is when to stop, but the bass player? When the song goes to the B-minor bridge after the second chorus, the bass has to go there, with authority and precision. You have to remember that you've just done the second chorus, and God help you if you got lost in the music for a moment and lost your place. So we'd had no rehearsal and our first gig was in a sold-out casino showroom. Straight into the fire. I can't say I hated it, but I can't say I enjoyed it either. We only did two gigs. A weekend. That was it. If we'd done two weeks of gigs and I'd had time to really acclimate, I might have really had a ball eventually, but this wasn't the situation.

Mind you, I didn't play badly. I've heard the show tapes. I didn't play perfectly. But I was in the pocket with Paul on the drums more often than not. I had practiced and practiced and I was as ready as I could have been for that gig. I wasn't suffering from overconfidence, but I was professional. I don't think I even drank or smoked pot before the shows.

However, I did see something backstage in the green room that I had never seen before and haven't seen since—a Mason jar full of pain pills, courtesy of somebody. A Mason jar like your grandmother used to store pickles in for the winter. When no one was in the room, I tugged my front pants pocket open and tipped the Mason jar into it. I was high for a week off that score.

Another thing I discovered that weekend was that I hate casinos: the noise, the gaudiness, and frankly the people. The staff was quite nice, but I caught a vibe, a low-level skeevy quality in a lot of the gamblers. Everything on the surface was fun and games and people having a blast, but you also got the sense that lives were being ruined in there. Of all the vices out there, I can at least be a snob about gambling. Never appealed to me. All the while we were there, taking limos, staying in opulent rooms and living and eating like kings, I never played a hand of blackjack, never played a slot machine, poker, keno, nothing. Never wanted to. I don't even understand what sort of buzz people get out of the experience.

But then, there are people who take pain pills for three days after spraining an ankle, and then let the rest of the bottle languish untouched in the back of the medicine cabinet for months or even years. I don't understand those people, either. I don't even think I like them.

* * * * * *

September 8, 2006

TONIGHT ON LENO!! Mariska Hargitay from *Law & Order SVU*, Ashley Stanfield from some Disney Channel show, a moron Nascar driver AND MUSIC FROM TODD SNIDER & THE NERVOUS WRECKS!!

I was 43 years old and I was Todd's rhythm guitarist. (No longer on bass, thank God.) And I was about to be on national television for the first time in my life. This had to be good. We rehearsed a lot the day before and I KNEW that song. I could play the right parts just like on the record, his new single: "Looking for a Job." I was never more ready for anything in my life. It was a great band: Doug Lancio on lead guitar, Paul Griffith on drums, Molly Thomas on fiddle, David Zollo on piano, Peter Cooper on bass and me on the trusty Telecaster I'd been playing for almost 25 years. I had a Fender Deluxe, a great amp for making controlled racket in the key of G.

For once I was sober. Todd had the big dressing room that was party central. It reeked of pot and refreshments abounded. Jack Daniel's, Heineken, Quervo, Cabernet Savignon, anything you wanted. And this was going on about an hour before the show. I stayed out of it. Completely. I didn't touch any weed, I didn't drink anything but Diet Coke all day.

When we went out there and played the song, I didn't make any wrong moves, I rocked, with good movement on the stage and guitar but careful not to overdo it. I was there to make Todd shine, nothing less and nothing more. The whole performance was great for everybody. We nailed it. Three minutes of terror metamorphosed as ecstasy.

The after-party was on the roof of our seriously ritzy hotel right off the Sunset Strip, a quick walk to the Viper Room. This was primo social- izing shit. Big Wigs in the music business were there. Pamela Des Barres even showed up. Later on, we watched the broadcast, all crammed into one room with people sitting on the floor, and it was wonderful. And then the problems started.

The guy I roomed with—who shall remain nameless—had an in- imitable talent for finding cocaine. He could score blow in Vatican City. He left the hotel on his quest and came back in a couple of hours with half an eight-ball.

"ALRIGHT, ROOMIE!!" I exclaimed at 3 a.m. when he returned from his reconnaissance-and-procurement mission. Thus began the all-nighter of watching TV and not much else. We had a pile on a coffee table and a convenient newspaper page to toss over it if anyone suddenly wanted to come in. Nobody else knew what we were doing. Nothing intruded on our drug fun. We were still buzzing from playing the Leno show. We had that Keith Richards feeling. We were in a luxury hotel, had just played on na- tional television. We were big-time for a moment. We were rock stars. And we felt so good about that, that we snorted some more. Four a.m. turned to 7 and there we were, my buddy and me, up all night on blow, talking about rock 'n' roll and Faulkner and coolness, our eyes getting redder and our bodies more achy from lack of sleep. And then came the crash.

Suddenly, my body reminded me that I hadn't eaten for a long while, and my blood sugar was about to go south in a big way. I put on my courtesy robe and took the elevator to the concierge and asked for two things: Could you please quickly find me a big bottle of orange juice and one or two bananas? I explained that it was a matter of life and death and in all seriousness I had to eat something. Soon. The dude at the desk came through, and I ate my wonderful banana and drank my juice, and moved closer to feeling like I wasn't going to die. But it was a drop in the ocean. I was already emaciated and pale. I wouldn't fully get my health back for the rest of the day.

I went back to the room and snorted more blow. We still had plenty, and I'd be back on that wagon trail all day and tonight as well. Todd was playing the Troubadour that night, and he was doing it solo acoustic, with special guest appearances by Molly on fiddle for one or two songs, and me backing him up on one song. I never learned the song. I listened to it several times on my iPod and figured I knew it well enough. I wasn't the guy I was yesterday, I didn't KNOW the song I was going to play at the Troubadour, for fuck's sake. I really didn't know anything but the bare bones of the tune and where my guitar freak-out was supposed to happen.

I was up in the dressing room with my roomie during Todd's open-ing few numbers, and going to the bathroom an awful lot. I was gacked to the gills when Todd beckoned for me to come up onstage to do our song. I followed his hands for the chord changes, tried not to be too sloppy, but then my lead break was an abortion and the performance never regained its vigor. The applause was generous from some parts of the sold-out crowd and tepid in other areas. I walked off the stage, really hoping to not make eye contact with anybody. I'd been so ON yesterday in Beautiful Downtown Burbank doing Leno, and now here I am a night later, gacked, unprepared, and I screwed the pooch. This was the Trou-badour in Los Angeles, and it was sold out to several hundred people I could have made some good impressions. But I didn't.

After Leno (and Letterman two weeks later), I did a few more shows with Todd and then it just kind of dried up, forever.

I'm not cut out to be a sideman. I'm a decent guitar player but I can't play the same thing twice in a row. I'm limited as a vocalist. I can sing Keith Richards harmonies, but that's about it. And besides, I'm nervous as hell doing a sideman gig, too afraid of screwing up to really enjoy things. There were several gigs with Todd where I was brought in to be the lead guitar player, the role Kimbrough held for many years. As a guitarist Will is up there with Albert Lee and Richard Thompson, and I was standing in shoes I couldn't fill, and everyone had to know it. In all the Todd gigs for which I played lead guitar, exactly one time did I play a guitar lead that excited whoops from the audience. You don't keep hiring a guy who plays exactly *one* badass lead over the course of a full dozen shows.

Then you have the cocaine. One of the most harrowing things about my cocaine experience (2006-2008) is remembering some of the things I said and did. I remember sending Todd a long email when I was gee-zed up one night, and the message was full of advice he hadn't asked for. That didn't go over too well. I was secretly snorting several times when I was on the road with him. I remember sitting behind him in the van and he said, "Tommy, you sound a little congested." It didn't sink in that he might have been on to me. There are lots of things I clearly see the meaning of now that didn't occur to me at the time.

I wonder if Todd feels the same way about potheads that I do. I don't trust them. I never have. I stayed stoned for decades and I still never trusted anyone else who behaved that way. Potheads let you down. They're late, they lose their place in the middle of songs, they stink, and they can't be trusted. The only reason I could smoke as much dope as I did was that I was the only human out of four billion who was special. Pot made the rest of the world stupid but certainly not me.

* * * * * *

Years after Dad became an ordained minister, and had his own church, Mom had an idea. She wanted to have a family devotional at dinnertime. There would be a Bible reading and a prayer, but Dad, a guy *who gave spiritual advice for a living,* shot the whole thing down. His response to Mom was classic.

"I don't see the point in praying just because it's dinnertime!"

* * * * * *

Saturday, December 31, 2011

Happy New Year. Almost. It's 10:19 p.m. I'm watching a *Lockup* marathon. I had my choice of several activities, and chose this, plopped on my ass in bed. Beth is over at the Kennadys' house. The church friends with the pool. Nathan is with her. He wants to stay up 'til midnight. I couldn't care less if you put me through a training course on how to care less. Happy ding dang New Year. May it be a year without onstage blackouts, or written warnings at work, or pilled-up rants, or driving 40 blocks up Central Park West on a blown-out tire rim, stoned as a bat at four in the morning, fun as that was.

* * * * * *

Skinny & Small

When I was a kid I was skinny and small
And skinny kids in my town they played ball
It was the little girls sat around with dolls
And that's how it was in my town when I was skinny and small
Skinny & small

They gave me a glove and stuck me in a field
Yelled at me to hit, yelled at me to steal
Yelled at me all damn day is how it'd feel
And that's how it was in my town when I was skinny and small

Eighth grade gym and jock strap humor
Always the subject of some ugly rumor
He can't play sports, he must be a fag
Stay away from him he's a drag

Ninth grade gym I couldn't climb the rope
Coach shook his head said there ain't no hope
This is a one-level and you can't compete
You don't think like an athlete

So I grew up tough, I grew up mean
My fists got hard, my wits got keen
I left that little one horse town
Gonna bring some ivory towers down

When I was a kid I was skinny and small
And skinny kids in my town they played ball
It was the little girls sat around with dolls
And that's how it was in my town when I was skinny and small
Skinny & small

He used to pitch no hitters and I warmed the bench
Gave me noogies and made me flinch
I came back to town with a big ass wrench
And said this is for the way you treated me
And I struck him on the head repeatedly
Repeatly

I caught up with the shortstop found out what he does
He's still livin' in town, he's the chief of the fuzz
The chief of the fuzz, at least he was
I shot him an hour ago

And now I'm runnin' through the woods quiet as a mouse
Only 50 yards from the coach's house
Hello? Anybody home?

When I was a kid I was skinny and small
And skinny kids in my town they played ball
It was the little girls sat around with dolls
And that's how it was in my town when I was skinny and small
Skinny & small

* * * * * *

What do you call a drummer in a three-piece suit?
    The defendant. . . . *the defendant.* Is this on?

heifer, ye shall be healed!!

I Thought I Was Fine

I thought I was fine, I didn't know
The choices were mine, I could have said no
Now I'm out driving with no peace of mind
People know better, I thought I was fine

I'd changed all my strings, they were all clear and bright
The stars were out shining, it was a beautiful night
I thought I could see, didn't know I was blind
Some folks applauded, I thought I was fine

My mother loves me, I've got some good friends
The road goes on forever and the party never ends
I've known destruction, women and wine
Last night was different, I thought I was fine

Fish gotta fly, birds gotta swim
The Lord had to die, I'll never be him
I know pretty soon, I'll be alone crying
I was laughing last night, I thought I was fine

My grandfather died, in the house that he built
He never knew pleasure, never knew guilt
He never touched liquor, never touched wine
I never did like him, he thought he was fine

You can tie one on, get a nice buzz
Tomorrow will dawn, it always does
I'll carry this fear in the front of my mind
It'll happen again, when I thought I was fine

* * * * * *

My parents' life in the 1940s is an amorphous one. Years have been lost to time and there is no one left to ask anymore.

I really don't know how and when it happened, but sometime in the mid to late 1940s Dad snared a preaching gig. And when that one went by the wayside, he learned of a need for a preacher in a rural Oklahoma town. J.C. and Lorene Womack, with the boy Waymond, hit the dusty road. Leaving everything they knew.

They set up a home. Their backyard was bordered with a barbed-wire fence. On the other side of that fence was a sizable herd of cattle. The perfect audience.

Dad practiced his sermons to the cows. I shit thee not. He'd be down at the fence, holding his written sermon in one hand and holding the other hand up in the air gesticulating in a churchy way, hollering to those cows about the Lord Jesus and His Orchestra. He would work up to a fever pitch, and then pull back for a quieter moment. Dad became a good preacher over the next few years and a lot of credit goes to his incessant practice in those years in Oklahoma, filling a bovine test audience with the Holy Spirit.

* * * * * *

January 14, 2012

About a year ago I got busted at Vanderbilt for lollygagging on the job, surfing the net, checking Facebook and basically doing anything but what I was supposed to be doing—coding those goddam infernal patient complaints. I was given a written warning and had my internet taken away except for the sites I needed to do my job. My productivity skyrocketed, and that's been noticed by my immediate supervisor, which is good—but I don't know how much the grand poobahs know of my uptick. I got my internet back after six months or so, and I don't know why, but I've never piped up about it.

So Dr. Hitchel—who busted me in the first place—walks past my desk now and then. He *never* came around before, but now when he does he sees if I'm doing anything frivolous. He doesn't say anything, but my butthole pucker would speak for the both of us. Then there's Dr. Kerns, Mr. Big, the *capo di tutti capi*. He hasn't liked me since I came in one day wearing a top hat. Beth says I'm paranoid. I say what else is paranoia but a healthy hypersensitivity to dark possibilities?

I have a record coming out, so in the morning I'll edit liner notes while a plumber from the Drain Doc comes over to unclog the pound of roast beef I tried to stick in the garbage disposal all at the same time. Then I'll go to work, and then I'll pick up Dan and Justin and go to play a benefit for mistreated children in Livingston, 100 miles east of Nashville. Hippie Jack's putting it on. It's an early gig. We'll be back home by 11. And then I'll sleep and then I'll go to work again, because that's what I do. I work for the man. Twenty-five years of gigs, 15 records, two books, six tours of Europe and I'm working for the man.

* * * * * *

I was a frat boy back in the day, if you can believe that. I was even vice president of the place. Sigma Phi Epsilon, Kentucky Delta Chapter, at Western Kentucky University. We were the most charming, eclectic fraternity on campus, far less aloof than the more moneyed enclaves up the hill. We had the best music by far. Other houses were blasting "Celebration" by Kool & the Gang and we were throwing down to the Ramones and Sleepy LaBeef. We were like the Animal House with less wanton destruction (but still some!). I was deeply ashamed of being a Greek in later years when I was putting on the local rock-star pose, but now it's safe to say that I have fond memories of that Sig Ep basement of ours, redolent with spilt beer and mildew. I danced with a lot of girls down there, and a few guys. (You had to be there.) I played my first rock 'n' roll gig ever down there. Government Cheese played its first gig there.

It was there I met the girl who would ultimately be the love of my life, Beth. The first thing that caught my attention was her eyes. She had dark, wildly expressive eyes—still does. Her cheeks were full, dimpled and sprayed with freckles. She looked like a mix of Buffy Davis and the lady with the torch at the beginning of old Columbia Pictures movies, down to the reddish-brown hair. I didn't even really register what her body looked like; I was fixated on her eyes. I'm still a face guy, just like with Tina in ninth grade—I can pretty much go with anything bodily so long as the face is right, so long as there isn't a third leg or anything. I thought she was foxy. I still do, over 30 years later, when I back up and appreciate her, which is sadly not often enough.

Beth Tucker, from Horse Cave, Kentucky. We started seeing each other, which continued off and on for two years or more. It would spark and sputter, mainly because she wasn't a loose woman and I liked loose women a lot. But I kept coming back to her, and one day in my last semester, the fall of '84, we hooked up for good. I just had a feeling about her. By the spring of '85, we were living together on the sly, neither set of parents wise to it.

I have really fond memories of that spring and summer of 1985 after we'd graduated. We were both working at radio stations, she as the news director of WBGN and I as the morning man at WLBJ, and we were living in a little two-room apartment in the back of a house on Chestnut Street. Whenever I think of the show *Moonlighting* I think of that old apartment, because that was a hip new show we would watch on our little black-and-white TV before turning in early, since we both had to work early. I would come home every day and strum my guitar and play along to R.E.M. records. It was a simple, innocent time. I remember watching Live Aid on that television before we turned it off and drove to Nashville to see Jay Leno play Zanies. It's funny how little things like that stick with you. It was just Beth and me, younger than we realized we were. Little children dressed up as adults.

Fond memories aside, I still had a lot of problems. I spent a lot of time depressed, sometimes severely. I was going to see a Dr. Burroughs in Hopkinsville, Kentucky, who was a minister in my dad's denomination. He owed Dad a favor and saw me for free. Once a week I'd take 45 minutes of two-lane state roads to go see him. That summer of '85, I went to what I didn't know would be our last meeting. We sat down in his office and right off the bat he laid something on me flat out.

"Tommy," he said, "I've been getting to know you for two years, and I have a fair assessment what lies beneath your depression and resentments. You're an alcoholic."

What? I was furious. After two years of talking over my fucked-up life, that's all he had to tell me? I'm an alcoholic? I've never wrecked a car, never been in a bar fight, never been arrested, never had anyone ELSE tell me I had a problem. What is this "alcoholic" shit?!

So I figured, I'll show him. And I stopped . . . everything! I stopped drinking. I stopped smoking pot. And that's all I had been doing so there wasn't anything else to quit, except for the Marlboro Lights and Folger's. I didn't quit them. If anything, I upped my intake. For the next year, 1985 to well into 1986, I was sober as a judge, utterly devoted to two things: Beth and getting Government Cheese off the ground.

When a three-room apartment opened up in the front of the house in September, we took it. That was where we would be for the next three years, through good and bad. That was where we would live while Government Cheese mushroomed, and I started drinking again, among other things.

* * * * * *

I don't know the details, but Mom and Dad and Waymond moved around the prairie to a new church every few years. (The record I can gather, so much as it's known, is that Dad never preached anywhere for very long.) They wound up in Texas at one point, and sometime in the 1950s they moved back to the real South and their own kind of people, winding up in Atwood, Tennessee, where Dad found himself installed at the Atwood Cumberland Presbyterian Church, and where my middle brother, Jerry, would be born on March 6, 1956. Three years, three months and seven days later, my sister Rhena was born, on July 13, 1959. (And exactly three years, three months and seven days later *again,* I was born.)

* * * * * *

How do you know when a Hoosier girl is on her period? She's only wearing one sock. How are keyboards like condoms? You lose a little feel but occasionally they're necessary. What's the last thing a drummer says before he leaves a band? Hey, guys, let's try one of my own songs! I got busted once for smuggling books into Indiana. The cops let me go because none of them could prove that they were books. What did the snail say when riding on the turtle's back? Whee!

12

it's always something

Dad was a good man who wouldn't harm a fly, but as we have seen, he was broody long-term over God knows what. He charmed visitors, but when they were gone, he went back into his own space. And I think people he worked with noticed it too, or traces of it, once they got to know him. He could be blunt, and tone-deaf to niceties, and of course when you pick your nose anywhere at any time, people make decisions about you.

But he was a good man. He was honest. He wasn't vindictive. Never conniving, never chasing skirts. He spanked us as kids but that's where it stopped. He never beat Mom up and he never, ever drank. He just had trouble finding people he could relax with outside the home, really relax, and really get to know. In his heart, some doors were shut.

One thing about him I inherited was that when he got a bee in his bonnet about something, he obsessed on it. Once he got the calling to preach back in the mid-forties, that's what he fixated on, and on, and on. Mom told me that Dad had decided he wouldn't ever feel right about his life until he could pastor a church. Until that happened, life was shit (and if Dad's life was shit, *everybody's* life was shit).

So then he got to be a preacher, and it was satisfying, but then he got *another* bee in his bonnet: he wasn't ordained, and he wanted to be. He didn't have a college degree; he didn't have the credentials to work the big rooms in an established Christian denomination with many branch churches around the land. So Dad became fixated on the fact that he needed a college degree, and until he got one, life was shit.

Part of the reason to get back to Tennessee was to be in close proximity to Bethel College in McKenzie, the official Bible college of the Cumberland Presbyterian Church. It was 1957 or '58, he was teaching high school and preaching two churches, one in Atwood and another somewhere else. He was in the volunteer fire department. And on top of all this, he was enrolled at Bethel, taking a full course load, all night classes. Mom did her best to raise Waymond and Jerry while Dad was always at one gig or another, or studying. And wouldn't you know it, he did it! Dad graduated with a B.A. and was ordained a Cumberland Presbyterian minister in 1960. The son of a bitch pulled off the impossible. And kudos to him.

I like to imagine he had a moment soon thereafter, when he was outside at night, looking up at the stars with his back arched and one hand holding a cigarette, and wondered what the hell he'd fixate on next.

* * * * * *

There was no sure route in my upbringing for me to grow up and play music for a living, but I managed it, and I've had hundreds and hundreds of incredible nights bopping around on a stage while people danced and cheered. When you're playing music on a stage, and it's going well, and you have an audience hanging on everything you do, you go to another place, and I've been there many times. One great night onstage can fill your mystic belly for weeks. So long as I have a good gig every so often, the offstage life as a regular schmuck is mostly bearable.

I love attention. I always have. And until I had a performance outlet for it, I was insufferable. In high school I never got invited to the same party twice. I was the comic who wasn't funny, the desperate kid. Now it's different. I have my gigs. I get my fix onstage and so when I'm off the boards I can blend into society without irritating everybody like in high school.

I have another way to get a fix, too. When my first book came out I got a whiff of people having that book on their nightstands, reading something where I put all the periods and commas and adjectives in their jewel-set places better than I could ever do with my singing voice and my playing fingers. It was a fulfillment I'd never known. Sure, my records had been on peoples' shelves before, but this time, with a book, it was different. As opposed to records, those books, they'll be on a shelf somewhere, often for a very long time, and you can just pick them up. You won't have to plug them in, you won't have to charge them up; they will live. And with books I can be onstage without leaving the house.

* * * * * *

The world needs another singer-songwriter like it needs somebody ringing your doorbell and slinging bleach onto your clothes. The world needs all its celebrities to perish in an orgiastic spiral of guns, drugs and violence. I believe you spend a day in Hell for each day you make money off the sacred Word of God on a redneck television station where the telethon never ends. I believe language was invented to replace weaponry. I believe I'll have another beer.

* * * * * *

It's April of 1999 and I'm 36 years old. I'm driving my GMC Jimmy through pissing, blowing, torrential rain from New York to Boston for a gig at the Kendall Café. I can't cut the engine off because the car's fucked and it might not restart. I fill up at gas stations with the engine running. Oh, and there's also a hole in the back passenger window. It's patched up with duct tape but the rain is seeping in all around it.

This is near the end of a tour that started bad and has gotten worse. I'm paired up with an Australian singer-songwriter named Steven Camden. The gigs were in good rooms but we haven't been drawing shit for audiences. I think the booking agent and manager might have put stars into Steven's eyes, that the gigs were going to be great and that the USA was ready for Steven Camden, and now, three weeks later, he's feeling like he's been sold a bill of goods. Me? I'm stoned. All the time. It's the only way to deal with it.

The Jimmy had quit the day before in Brooklyn, where I'd bunked up in Park Slope with Scott McClatchy, who plays with Top Ten some, and his wife Laura. I put my key in the ignition and nothing happened. Thus began the litany of finding a tow truck and a mechanic in the cruelest city in the world. I called a service called Mr. Rescue. A short, buff guy who spoke in movie Brooklynese showed up in short order with a tow truck, with just enough time for me to lock the keys in the car. Short Buff Guy just happened to have a four-foot-long 4x4 piece of lumber in his truck. God knows why. Apparently they're useful. There was no choice but to smash one of the windows. When I saw Buffy put that 4x4 through the back passenger glass, I wanted to throw up. He then went around, threw the wood back into the tow truck, opened the door of my GMC, reached in on the driver's side, turned the key, put it in neutral and then did that chains-and-jacks shit that you do when you're going to tow a car. Then Buffy and I took a ride all the way to Coney Island, where the mechanic was. I left the GMC there, took a cab back to Scott and Laura's in Brooklyn and somehow in my completely freaked-out state managed to make the gig in Manhattan that night at the Lakeside Lounge, and drink prodigious amounts of Maker's Mark.

At eight this morning I wasn't just hung over, I was raped and mummified. But I roused myself on a gloomy, rainy morning and called the mechanic. I don't even remember what we talked about. The GMC, I guess. I wound up in Coney Island either by cab or train or magic carpet, I don't fucking know. All I knew was there I was at the mechanic's and there's this old guy with a beard and a turban talking to me.

They'd gotten the Jimmy running. Buffy was there. "Mr. Womack," he implored, "I strongly recommend you not take this car on the road today." The fossil in the turban waved him off and spoke to me. "Is your starter," he said in broken English, "but here what you do." Reaching into the engine, he pulled a cap off something to reveal a valve of some sort. Then he took an aerosol can of some chemical probably banned in the U.S. and he sprayed it directly on the valve. "Now, you start her up." And it started right up. Simple enough to do, it seemed. Looney Tunes, too! Spraying some unknown, probably flammable chemical into the innards of my engine. Buffy begged me again. "Mr. Womack, please give us a day to fix your starter properly." It was Sunday and they couldn't get parts. "No, thank you," I said, "I have to be in Boston tonight. The show must go on."

So I picked up Steven in the city, where he'd been staying with a friend, and that's when the rain started to pick up, which leads us to now, dealing with interstate traffic, reading MapQuest directions off of rain-spotted paper, and listening to the howls of wind whistling through the duct-taped window hole and into a vehicle we can't shut off. I rolled a joint at a fill-up. My last one. The bag is empty. It's not going to be good running out of pot at this juncture in the tour, but that's the way it's gonna be. I drive on, both my and Steven's nerves on edge. I'll light up the joint, take two big hits and stub it out, over and over, and now it's looking a little small. My right thumb and the tip of my forefinger are black and burned. I smell like five reggae bands rolled into one. I don't really notice it. It's just how everything around me smells. All the time.

The rain doesn't let up, we don't get any brief lighter spells, we just get buckets and buckets. It keeps coming. We hit Boston, and that's when we discover that the MapQuest directions have been composed by an autistic gibbon.

We find ourselves in Cambridge like the directions say, with one last turn to make before the Charles River. Trouble is there IS no one last turn before the river. We cross the river on the long bridge three times in the search for that left turn, and my blood is beginning to boil. These are the days without smartphones, or GPS. All I have is this wet piece of paper, and it's getting close to show time. For an hour, we drive around Cambridge, looking for any left turn that might be the right one. We find a convenience store, and outside it, a pay phone. It's piss-pouring rain as I pull the Jimmy up as close to the phone I can get. Cupping the number of the club on a piece of paper in my hand, I hunch my shoulders and exit the driver's-side door. I'm instantly drenched. I leap to the phone with my number and a quarter at the ready, pick up the receiver, AND IT FALLS APART IN MY HANDS! Into three pieces that hang down loose on the phone cable! THIS IS NOT HAPPENING! God! What are you doing to me here?!

I get back in the driver's seat wetter than water itself, and I start punching the dashboard with my fist. Over and over I punch that dashboard until I'm tired, and Steven is getting seriously frightened of me.

Long story short, we find the club, but not in time to play. We find a space in a parking garage, and, after a deep breath, we shut off the engine, and run across the street through the goddam rain. We walk into the Kendall Café and take opposite corners, Steven and I. It's time for a little "me time," I guess. I find a table, sit down with a double Maker's, rest my elbows on the table, cradle my head in my hands and start to sob. How bad do I want to play these godforsaken shows? Is the high of an audience worth it? Am I ever going to get anywhere? Am I never going to just wake up and accept that it's not going to happen for me? I sob and find no answers.

Two friends of mine are there. They invite us to stay with them. We can follow them home. We go to the Jimmy, open the hood, take the cap off the valve, spray the aerosol poison on it, replace the cap, and she starts right up! Take that, Buffy.

say, little girl . . .

Mom was walking to school one sunny day when she was about eight years old. Coming up the road the other way was an old man that Mom recognized as a preacher, maybe from Cabot. As they approached each other, he spoke.

"Well, hey there, little girl."

"Hey," Mom said.

They looked at each other for a moment and the preacher rubbed his chin and cogitated about something.

"Say, little girl," he drawled, "Chloe Waters, by gum it's gotta be. You his daughter?"

"Yes sir."

The preacher threw his head back and laughed. He laughed long and hard. Tears were coming to his eyes. Mom wondered what was so funny. "Little girl," the preacher said, "I knowed your father when he was younger than you. And I told him there and then that he was so ugly that if he ever found a woman who would take up with him, I'd marry 'em for free!" And with that, the preacher walked on down the road, and Mom walked on to school.

* * * * * *

Mom was a good woman, a very good woman. She never had anything but the best of intentions. Her whole life was for Jesus and her family.

She did the best she could with the tools she had. She was always, always very sweet to me.

She was also deeply unhappy, clinically depressed in an age before it was much recognized and treated. All the wounds that had been dealt to her—you'd think she would have toughened up, but it actually made her more sensitive. Her feelings were easily hurt, and if she had a tragic flaw at all, it was that she never forgot a slight, never got over what she perceived as an insult or a thoughtless act. Her whole being was infused with grudges she had held from the day her father told her she was the ugliest thing he'd ever seen. And then the douchebag preacher had to weigh in, too. She grew up hurt, and she stayed hurt: a wedding in a general store with no bouquet to toss, the honeymoon pedicure, much more. It had all added up. And if she needed anything fresh and new to feel hurt about, she could always count on Dad for something sooner or later.

Even with all the slights and insults she'd endured, Mom never did anything to avenge anything, ever. "Two wrongs don't make a right" she'd always tell me. It just stayed in her gut. It came out through the ulcers in her mouth that she drank the Knox gelatin for.

She had worked her ass off her entire life, first in the cotton fields, then as a housewife, mother and preacher's wife. She'd raised one boy to the age of 13 and then suddenly she had three more kids, a whole new brood. She kept the house clean, cooked, did the dishes, gave us baths, gave affection and filled in all the parental gaps whenever Dad was watching *Barnaby Jones.*

She had me when she was 40, when she was already tired. And Dad was tired, too. They didn't deserve me, fixing my own bowls of Cheerios with four spoonfuls of sugar at age four, pinging off the walls and always needing to be the center of attention. One of my early memories is of Mom always needing to lie down on her bed in the middle of the day. At 44 she was already tired deep down in her bones.

✱ ✱ ✱ ✱ ✱ ✱

It's the summer of 1966, I think. I don't really know. I'm just a tiny little boy. I'm riding in the front seat of our '64 white Plymouth Fury with Dad driving on my left side and Mom sitting to my right. There are no such things as seatbelts. Nobody thinks a thing about it. We're going on a ride somewhere. Mom and I are talking and Dad is driving and flicking Camel ashes out the window. Jerry and Rhena are in the back seat arguing about something, then laughing about something. Kids.

I say to Mom, "One, two, three, four . . ." Good, she says, keep going! I say, "Five, six, seven, eight, nine . . ." That's good! Keep going. "Ten . . .

eleven . . . ummm . . . TWELVE!" I couldn't do any more. I hit the wall. But Mom tells me I'm such a smart boy. Then I say, "John, Paul, George . . . and . . . and . . ." "Reeeee . . . ," Mom hints. "Ringo!" I holler. That's right, she says, you're Momma's little sweet boy. We ride on.

* * * * * *

Sunday, February 5, 2012

I've just got sunshine blowing out of my ass. I'm such a shining beacon of goddam optimism. Everything's fine. Flippety fucking fine!

This past week I spent five hours a day at Vanderbilt coding those god-fucking-damn shit-ass patient complaints, wishing I had the balls to run in front of a Mack truck. I didn't have gigs this weekend, and so I watched so much television my intestines are radioactive. Life. It's all about the journey. The grand, glorious, ding-dang journey.

I have a new record. It's going to come out, I'm going to play in a store here in town, I'm going to play a choice few gigs in select markets, and then life's going to settle back into the fondue of shit-mousse it always is.

But Tommy, thinking that way just conjures the very negative eventualities you verbalize! Fuck you. You'd do well to keep your filthy mitts off my eventualities. I've been on this merry-go-round a long fucking time. You either build your hopes up and get dashed, or you steel yourself for the disappointment. Take your pick. *But Tommy, you have thousands of fans!* Fuck you. Don't you wave my fans in my face. I hate my fans. I wish I could hang them all up in my smokehouse, have smoked-fan sausage next Thanksgiving, where I'll carve the fan roast and ask God to bless my little charming fucking family I'm so fucking thankful for, this whole shit-pot of thankful blessedness, that I could vomit rainbows and piss diamonds. I'm so happy. I'm so fucking shit-ass happy! Shoot me, please!

* * * * * *

It's February 18th, 2010, in Nashville. February sucks. I just got home from my job on that campus and I don't even feel like saying its name. I got some mail. It's an envelope that feels like there's a card inside. I open the envelope. Sure enough a card, and a check; in other words, a merch order. One of many that say, "Please send me a Cheese Chronicles. Somebody borrowed mine and I never got it back." Good deal. Twenty bucks is twenty bucks. Without looking at the check, I read the card. "*Dear Tommy, blah blah we met once at South By Southwest years ago . . . yadda yadda . . . I've started the Henry Darger Memorial Endowment because he is the world's most unrecognized genius. You are the first recipient of this award. I hope this check helps you breathe a little easier. Your work is very important to me. No publicity please. Sincerely, Bob R---.*" *It's a check for ten thousand dollars.*

I keep my cool. I do attract crazy people; I am a freak magnet of the first order. Soooooooo . . . I'll deposit it tomorrow and we'll just see, won't we.

It'll clear. I'll be $10,000 richer. I'll buy a pedal board, I'll buy Beth a Kitchen Aid mixer. I'll be in a good place for a while, or at least ten thousand paces closer to it.

* * * * * *

Tuesday, February 21, 2012

Today is the release date of my new record. *(Now What!)* Things are going very well with it. *The New Yorker* did a piece on it, which is amazing. I was in the top five most-added records on the Americana charts this week. And I played a triumphant gig at Grimey's record store this evening to a pretty damn packed store.

Yesterday I did three interviews, two where the reporters came to my house and one where a radio DJ called me up and had me on the air. There was another radio interview the day before. *American Songwriter* magazine gave the record four stars. *Nashville Scene* magazine made my record-store appearance one of the top Critics' Picks of the week. I did an interview for *The Tennessean* last week. I have over $500 in pre-orders via the web, which is hardly a lot compared to bigger artists, but for me it's Five Hundred Goddam Dollars.

I go to the Folk Alliance convention in Memphis tomorrow and play several showcase gigs and hobnob with music-biz folks and performers both, which is always fun. I have a meeting with my English booking agent Friday morning before I leave. Then Friday night I'm playing Bowling Green in Lisa Oliver Gray's band. Then Saturday night is a night of Clash with Tommy Gun at the Basement, and then Sunday night I play in Louisville with Lisa. She'll do a set of her stuff with my band backing her and then I'll do a set with the same band. Then Monday is another radio interview, Thursday the 2nd is a gig in Oxford, Mississippi, opening for Blue Mountain, then Saturday the 3rd is the official record-release gig, again at the Basement. Then the week after THAT Lisa and I take off for an eight-day tour of Louisiana and Texas, winding up at the SXSW

convention, where I aim to redeem myself for last year's pilled-out deba-
cle. Later in the month are two gigs with Marshall Chapman and I don't
know what's after that. Sometimes it's fun being me, on the condition that
I drive a lot and carry guitar amps around.

* * * * * *

I was in sixth grade; it was the fall of 1973. I was almost 11 years
old, and Mom and I were coming back home from the grocery store.
"Mom," I asked, as she drove us down Princeton Pike, "does Dad like
me?" After a silence, I added, "I don't think he likes me."

Mom sighed. That was a common beginning of Mom's saying
something. There would be the sigh, and then she would talk. "Well, of
course he does, Tom! Dad . . . (sigh) . . . likes you."

"I don't think he does," I said.

"Son," she said, driving into the late-afternoon sun, "you don't
know how many times you've said something funny at home and then
your Daddy would repeat what you said to folks at church or at church
elders' meetings and he would slap his knee laughing about whatever
it was you came up with." "Well," I mused, "he doesn't seem to pay
attention when I say anything, ever. He really does that? Repeats things
I say to other people?" "He sure does," Mom said.

Two or three afternoons later, I was riding in the front passenger
seat again; only this time it was Dad driving. I needed some loose-leaf
paper for a school notebook. We went to Happy's Office Supply and
picked up some and headed back towards home.

Dad was wearing a hat and had his tie on still from working at
churchy stuff all day. He no longer looked like a Kennedy-assassination
movie extra. This was the '70s, and he now had a pair of hip wire frames
like everybody else had, and the '70s wide polyester double-knit lapels.
He was driving like he always did: right hand on the wheel, left hand
flicking Camel ashes out the window.

"Boy," he said, smoke drifting from his mouth as he spoke.

"Yeah?" I said.

"I like ya."

We didn't say a word the rest of the trip home. I was content with it.

* * * * * *

You hear the one about the Hoosier penis transplant? His hand rejected
it. THANK YOU NASHVILLE! Try the veal.

the *rolling stoned* interview

Monday, April 9, 2012

CATCHING UP WITH T WIGGY
By Bucky Goldstein

Fido is a noisy, popular coffee and food shop in Hillsboro Village in Nashville. It's not the ideal place for an interview, I thought as I tested my handheld voice recorder, sitting at my table with a steaming mug of Arabica blend on a sunny spring morning, but I know Tommy, I know he talks in a loud voice, and as he warms to the subject at hand I trust he'll vocally chainsaw through the din around us.

He was on time and lurched toward me with a deportment that told me that maybe the only way he managed his punctuality was to forswear any hygienic upkeep. The snap-brim hat hid the greasy locks, the loose leather jacket (on a sunny warm day) hid his slight frame. He wore a 36-hour shadow across the bottom half of his face.

To be fair, though, he DID have his act together—his musical act. His record was out, he was getting great reviews, and he was playing great shows. Or so I've heard.

Tommy sat down and shook my hand while his other hand held on to his own porcelain cup of coffee, the resultant gyrations spilling coffee all over his pants. "Ahh, shit." He grinned, "Did I get any on you?" As I assured him there was no harm done, he pulled some sort of blue pill from his shirt pocket, sat it down on the table and crushed it with the bottom of his cup, turning it into powder. With no compunction about witnesses, he scooped the powder into four lines of blue, pulled a two-inch piece of drinking straw out of the same shirt pocket, leaned over the table and snorted the four lines in rapid succession. He smiled at me. "Rule number 37 about taking drugs," he said in a morning-coffee voice, "hide in plain sight."

"I used to deliver interoffice mail all over Vanderbilt's campus," he says, "walking up and down all the sidewalks. So one day, when I was headed out of Calhoun Hall with my mailbag to start my rounds, on the front steps I pulled out a big joint and fired it up. I smoked on it all the way to the campus post office, stubbed it out on my shoe, put it in my pocket, stinking like hell, went in, picked up some mail, dropped some off, went back out and in front of the student center, fired up the joint again and walked all the way to Kirkland Hall, taking the sidewalks, nodding hello to people, and nobody noticed anything at all. I stubbed and relit that joint a couple more times on my rounds before I was done with it, stoned as a bat and stinking."

So what about the pill? "That was a 10 milligram hydrocodone. Want one? No? Good, 'cause I don't share." So with that bit of homage to Keith Richards's interview prep, I wrestled control and the interview properly began.

BUCKY: "So, how was Folk Alliance?"

TOMMY: "Yeah, Memphis, yeah, the Folk Alliance festival. Picture the Radisson Hotel and Convention Center in downtown Memphis. Nice place. What they do is they block out four whole floors of hotel rooms, like, from the 16th to the 20th floor. Now, every one of those rooms on every one of those floors is rented out by some different organization tied to the folk music/Americana/singer-songwriter world—booking agencies, record labels, managers, promoters, retail outlets, magazines, etcetera, etcetera. What happens is that each of these rooms hosts six or seven acts a night, from like 7 p.m. to 2 a.m. The acts are sometimes solo guys or girls, sometimes duos, sometimes groups, and they all play in the hotel rooms! No microphones! No amplifiers! It's the great equalizer. Nobody rides for free.

"So, you'll play, say, Room 1724 at 8 p.m., the Girlilla Marketing room. Only so many people can fit in these rooms. They'll be seated on the beds generally. You quickly realize how much floor space in a hotel room the beds take up. I don't know if I ever played a Folk Alliance gig for more than 10 people. Where are you gonna put 'em?

"So you do your gig there, seven or eight songs, and then you have to boogie because your 9:15 show in the Radio Free Canada room (Room 1911) is imminent. You go from the quiet confines of the hotel room to the Londinium street chaos that is the corridor. It's gridlock in the hallways. Ten cute young female folkies going this way with their guitars on their backs, three Hayes Carlls and two guys with bass fiddles going that way, two suits and a drunk DJ against the wall. You can't wait for the elevator; you'll be waiting until Sunday. You wade in the crowd for the fire escape stairs where all the smokers are packed like sardines out there, and you walk the two flights up to the 19th floor. You find 1911 and stash your guitar in their bathroom, maybe help yourself to the deli tray if there is one, maybe catch a little of whoever is playing at the moment. It's all your friends playing. You see more of your friends at these festivals than you do when you're all home, because we're never all home at the same time. And it's weird how the sound goes. The hallways are loud as fuck, but the minute you're in one of the rooms you can hear a pin drop. You really appreciate the work that goes into the architecture; and I suppose that also they design these places to cover up sex noises. Either way, it's a striking nuance.

"Now that's just the hotel rooms. There's a whole other scene going on down in the lobby and on the mezzanine. Down there in the Peabody Room or the Delta Room, or the Whatever Room, will be the "official" showcases for all the performers, a proper 30- to 45-minute performance under kinder conditions, i.e, P.A. and lights, and an audience in actual chairs, not reclined on beds like Romans at a banquet.

"This year I wasn't a full-fledged participant. I didn't officially showcase. I had a one-day badge, which was all I wanted. But Sack wanted me to show my face and play some tunes for the peeps and the movers and the shakers, so I drove the three hours to Memphis and stayed in the same Motel 6 she always puts me in when we go down to this thing. No way can I afford to actually stay at the Radisson where the convention is. You know why Motel 6 says they'll leave the light on for ya? That's because roaches run to hide."

B: "So you were there on Thursday, February 23rd, and early Friday the 24th. Is that correct?"

T: "Yes, your honor, that is correct."

B: "And then you went straight from Memphis to Bowling Green, Kentucky, did you not?"

T: "Yes, I did. I left after a breakfast meeting between me, Sack and Bob Paterson, my booking agent in the U.K. That sort of meeting will get your enthusiasm up for what you're doing. Music-biz meetings are always great rosy-glasses type of 'pump you up' exercises.

"So yeah, I drove to Nashville, stopped at home, put all my acoustic guitar gear in the house and schlepped all my electric gear out to the car—two guitars, the Strat and the Tele, the pedal board, the amp, the speaker cabinet, all the cables, the extension cord. Let me tell you, the only thing good about the electric gigs is the music itself. Carrying the gear sucks balls."

B: "How did you feel going into Lisa's gig?"

T: "I was nervous. I really wanted to do well."

B: "How did the gig go?"

T: "It went fine, I reckon. I don't remember any serious fuckups."

B: "So, were you using during all this?"

T: "Was I USING?" *(Laughs.)* "Are we using the rehab terminology now? No, I had my prescription Xanax and the only dabble with booze came in Memphis in the Red Beet Records bathroom about midnight, when I was locked in there alone, relieving myself and there were about seven liquor bottles on the lavatory counter. I uncapped the Maker's Mark and drank down two or three good healthy slugs. Cleared my spiritual boogers out!"

B: "But you didn't drink in Bowling Green."

T: "No, Bucky. The Twisted Tap Tavern doesn't have liquor in the bathrooms."

B: "Okay, that takes us up to Saturday the 25th. Your Clash cover band, Tommy Gun, played in Nashville at the Basement. How was that?"

T: "That was a lot of fun, Bucky. That gig was a vacation, practically. No strumming an acoustic in a hotel room, no playing backup guy, just playing the loud and fast music of my youth, pretending to be Joe

Strummer, and appreciating anew how much hard work goes into being Joe Strummer, or trying to be him anyway."

B: "Did you drink that night?"

T: "Are we gonna go over that for every day we're catching up on?" *(Pause.)* "Truth be told, I don't know if I drank that night or not."

B: "So what you're telling me, Tommy, is that you may have drunk on the quiet so often that the episodes of falling off the wagon don't stick out in your memory now. It was something you were regularly doing."

T: "I gotta go to the bathroom!"

Tommy rose, grabbed his coffee cup and stormed off, leaving me to wonder why he would take his coffee cup with him to the restroom. He returned, and as he sat back down I saw that his coffee cup was significantly fuller than it had been, and redolent of merriment.

B: "Your cup wafts nicely of Irish cream now."

T: "Where were we?"

B: "Sunday, February 26th. What do you remember?"

T: "Lisa and I played dual record-release shows in Louisville, at Uncle Slayton's. We used the same band, along with Michael Webb on keyboards. It was a good gig. Lisa got a lot of people out. She's from Elizabethtown, an hour south, so she had a lot of old friends there. I had some of my fans there. Not many, though. I don't draw flies there. Government Cheese used to own Louisville. I can't get arrested."

B: "Did you have a good time, at least?"

T: "It was okay. The music was good. I had an anger attack earlier at sound check. The soundman there is a real dick and I have trouble with dicks. My 'fuck you' button is set on a 60-second delay, so that I never think to say it until the proper moment's gone, and I find myself with just a little more bottled-up rage than usual."

B: "Moving on. Monday, February 27th. The Mando Blues Radio Show taping."

T: "Yeah." *(Sighs.)* "Not me at my best. I bought a half pint of Myers's rum on the way to the station, drank it all, did the show, played about four or five songs with Lisa singing with me, then split from the stage very fast and went behind the curtain to throw up. Sack came back to check on me; I told her about the pot I'd just smoked, didn't say anything about the rum. I wound up going back to the mike and doing a pretty bang-up version of 'Pot Head Blues.' Mary said it was the best version she'd ever heard me do."

B: "What about the next two days, the 28th and 29th?"

T: "I didn't do a thing except work the day gig and hang out on the bed with my laptop. I mean, I don't actually *remember* doing that, but that's what I did, I guarantee you. It's all I ever did, either working on this book or surfing message boards."

B: "Okay, Thursday, March 1st, Proud Larry's, Oxford, Mississippi."

T: "Opened for Blue Mountain, and it was really nice to see 'em, Cary and Laurie; they're good people. I had a good Cajun pasta and sausage dish and Dan and I played for a few uninterested people. The club runs late. A few people seemed to like us, though. When I went into '90 Miles an Hour Down a Dead-End Street' that quieted the room pretty well. It's an a capella rap and it always gets folks' attention. Other than that it was a pretty painful gig. You just can't get over a room full of talkers with an acoustic guitar and a bass when they don't know you and don't care."

B: "Did you drink?"

T: "On the quiet, yeah."

B: "Did Dan know?"

T: "I was pretty sneaky with it. If he knew, he didn't give any indications of it. I was shooting quick tequila shots at the bar when he wasn't around, and then getting the hell away from the bar with my big glass of Diet Coke in my hand as quick as I could do the shot."

B: "How much was your bar tab?"

T: "Fifty dollars, exactly."

B: "How much were you paid for the gig?"

T: "One hundred fifty dollars."

B: "How much did you pay Dan?"

T: "Forty, I think."

B: "What were your management and booking commissions?"

T: "Thirty-seven fifty."

B: "So how much did that leave you?"

C: "Twenty-two dollars and fifty cents."

B: "What do you estimate your gas expense to have been?"

T: "Probably around forty dollars."

B: "So you lost around twenty dollars to travel five hours from home to play a gig."

T: "Yep." *(He lifted his cup to his lips, looked at it a moment, then set it down on the table without taking a sip.)*

B: "Was it worth it? Did you at least get a pleasant, jolly drunk out of it?"

T: "I didn't get drunk at all! That's alcoholism for you. I can drink a fifth one day and not get smashed, drink a shot the next day and be off the rails. You don't know if you're going to get heads or tails; you just flip a coin."

We sat and I nursed my coffee a little, then I got up for a refill. When I came back, Tommy was staring sullenly out the window, and his cup was empty.

B: "Okay, Saturday, March 3rd. Your big night. The record release party at the Basement. How was it?"

T: "Great. Good crowd. The band was good. We had the debut of the brass section. Everybody seemed to like it."

B: "Did you drink?"

T: "Yep."

B: "How much?"

T: "Four shots of Maker's."

B: "Sneaking them?"

T: "Of course! You see I have a special power. I can be invisible at a bar. No one can see me go over to it. It's magic!"

B: "Did you smoke any weed?"

T: "One toke."

B: "Did any of that help?

T: "It helped me forget some lyrics."

B: "So was your performance subpar?"

T: "I don't think it was *way* subpar. Everybody seemed to like it, the band included, but I could have been better."

B: "Does that bother you?"

T: "Bothers the hell out of me."

B: "Does it ruin the memory of the gig for you?

T: "Yep . . . yep . . . it does."

B: "Then why did you do it? Why do you do things to yourself that you know are coming to no good end?"

T: *(Snaps.)* "I don't know. I just don't frickin' know. I guess I just wanna *feel* something."

B: "What do you want to feel?"

T: "Joy, I reckon. Joy."

B: "Did you get away with drinking all that whiskey?"

T: "I thought I had, until the end of the night, when Sack asked me if I was alright to drive. I heard a toilet flush in my head when she asked me that."

B: "How did that make you feel?"

T: "Let's find a couch, talk about my toilet training."

B: "The question still stands."

T: "I swore up and down to her that I wasn't drinking, but I'm sure she smelled it. I don't know what stunk more, the whiskey or the dishonesty. She doesn't like me lying to her."

B: "Tommy, when you lie to somebody, they remember that. Forever. You blow that person's trust in you; it can take a lifetime to get it back, if you ever do at all."

T: "Yeah. I've been married nineteen years. I have a PhD in blowing trust out of the water."

B: "Your next show was the following Thursday, wasn't it?"

T: "If you say so."

B: "The Station Inn, with Marshall Chapman and Matraca Berg. How was that?"

T: "That one was good. It's an honor to play with them. I mean, Matraca's in the Country Songwriters' Hall of Fame and Marshall is, well, Marshall! And I stayed out of the booze."

B: "During the show."

T: "Yeah, during the show."

B: "What was the format?"

T: "Writers in a row on the stage. I played a song, then Matraca played one, then Marshall, then me again. Matraca's married to Jeff Hanna of the Nitty Gritty Dirt Band. He got up and did 'Mister Bojangles' and I got to sit in. That was really neat."

B: "I would say so."

T: "That's what I love about this town. So many neat and talented people to rub shoulders with. I can't get enough of that."

B: "Where did you go after the show?"

T: *(Squinting.)* "Why do you ask?"

B: "I hear things."

Tommy paused and gave me a look like a dog caught chewing the bedding.

T: "Okay, I went across the street to a bar and had two drinks."

B: "What did you drink?"

T: "What does it matter?"

B: "Just a nice little detail for the article. Readers love detail."

T: "Myers's rum. It's good stuff."

B: "How did that make you feel?"

T: "Like a drinker. It was a real swanky bar in a new strip of buildings across the street, real modern looking, lots of young people inside, enough of 'em to make me feel good and old, y'know."

B: "The next night was Friday, March 9th. New Orleans, right?"

T: "Right!" *(Tommy spat on the floor, disgusted.)*

B: "So tell me about it."

T: "New Orleans sucked. It sucked bad."
    "First of all, we had a ten-hour drive to get there. The club was a place called Flora Bon Tons. Make sure you write that down. I want

that club name in the article. That place can French-kiss my ass. Fuckin'
assholes from hell. Backbiting, backstabbing two-faced bunch of shit-
asses. Fuck them! FUCK them! Assholes . . ."

B: "I guess it was a bad gig?"

T: "I get pissed off all over again just thinking about it.
     "Okay, like I said, ten-hour drive, right? We drag-ass into the club.
Paul Sancious was opening up and he had a club full of people and he
was going down well. He saw me walk by him and smiled from the
stage. He gave me several props during his show. 'Make sure to stay
and see the great Tommy Womack!' Stuff like that. Oh, did I mention
Lisa was with me? She was with me, drove all the way down. Lisa has
to drive. Can't stand to not be driving, and that's fine by me.
     "So we ordered some pizza and ate it. Lisa's going to the bar to get
me Diet Cokes, so I don't have to get near the bar, and Paul's playing
and everything's fine, or at least as fine as it's going to be when you've
spent ten hours on the road just to get to the gig. And Paul finishes up
and I'm thinking, well, at least the gig's going to be pretty good. There's
people here, I'll probably move some merch, just gotta do a pro show,
y'know, and I can do that.
     "Then Paul leaves—and he TAKES EVERYBODY WITH HIM!
Everybody! Everybody splits! The club goes from full to ten people,
six of 'em to see me and four of 'em dead-set on talking through my
whole show! And those four people sat closer than anybody else. And
they weren't just talking; they were talking *loud!* Two guys and two
girls, dressed to the nines, drinking martinis at the end of the bar closest
to me. The guys kept going to the bathroom I swear every five minutes.
Now chicks go to the bathroom together, but not guys; I've snorted
enough coke to know what that means. Assholes! Talk, talk, talk!
     "I got pissed-er and pissed-er. And my last tune was 'Alpha Male
& the Canine Mystery Blood,' and when I sang the line about people
talking while I'm singing I was trembling with rage and stared a hole
through those people. Oh man, I was mad. Ten hours in the car . . . for
THIS??!!
     "I finished the tune, six people applauded, and I said, 'Thank you!
Those of you who were fucking listening!' and I stormed off the stage
and went to the bathroom to cool off.
     "I said to myself, it's gigs like that that just make you want to up
and quit. Just up and quit.
     "You know what's worse, one of my executive producers, Matt
Byrd, was there. What a gig for him to have to see. It just made me sad.

He followed me into the bathroom and told me how sorry he was about those yapping cokeheads, like it was his fault or something.

"I packed up the guitar and Lisa got paid, and the club-owner lady spoke to me and she was, if not quite apologetic, at least very nice and understanding. And I was slowly calming down. So we gave Matt and his wife a ride to their hotel, and then we headed off to our Motel 6 all the way on the other side of Lake Pontchartrain, and we got some sleep.

"So the next day I'm all cooled down and we get some breakfast and head off to Pasadena, Texas, to play Kenny Pipes' Almost Austin house concert series. We had a radio stop before that and it was at noon, so we had to get up early and hit the road. I was glad not to be hungover.

"We were zipping past bayous when my phone buzzed with a text. It was Sack, and the text read, 'So I see you had to shit the bed last night. Very nice. Thanks.'

"Everything went slow-motion all of the sudden. I was gobsmack stunned. I started trembling. You think I was furious the night before, now I was furious and stunned at the same time. What kind of text was that! I was convicted without a trial and hung out to dry like a wet, angry gym sock. I was foaming at the mouth.

"I got on the phone to Sack and for, I believe, the first time in my life, I full-fledged *yelled* at her! She didn't want to hear it, which made me even madder, because I'd certainly acquiesced to her dressing me down on more than one occasion.

"Turns out the two-faced, club-owning cunt had sent a Tolstoy screed of a midnight email to Mary, calling me an asshole and taking the side of the talkers. She couldn't say anything to *me,* apparently, but behind the safety of a modem she could let fly at Sack. She said I'd improvised a line about people talking while I'm singing, just to be an asshole; to which I say she deliberately hadn't listened to the record we sent her, because that line's in the fucking goddam recorded version for damn good reasons!

"I gave the phone to Lisa when it was apparent Mary wasn't going to listen to anything I had to say so long as I was saying it louder than a jet airplane, and Lisa backed up my side of the story. I shouted, 'Tell her to email Matt!'

"You know, Bucky, if I hadn't had Lisa and Matt there, Mary wouldn't have believed me. She would have believed the backstabbing club owner. It would have been my word against hers, and Mary would have believed the club owner."

B: *(After a pause.)* "Trust."

T: "Yeah . . . trust. I'd lied so much to her and got called on it so many times that my word isn't worth much with her."

B: "So how did the rest of that swing go? You went on to Texas, right?"

T: "Yeah, Texas. Pasadena. Played on the radio, went to Kenny's house, took a nap in his waterbed. Drank his cough syrup. Played the gig."

B: "How was the gig?"

T: "Half full. And the other half was empty."

B: "How much of Kenny's cough syrup did you drink?"

T: "Almost all of it."

B: "How did that make you feel?"

T: "Happy, at least at the moment. Later I was afraid Kenny'd have a coughing fit someday and reach for his medicine, and there wouldn't be any there, and I feel bad about that."

B: "Then you went on to Dallas?"

T: *(Groaning.)* "Yeah."

B: "What happened there?"

T: "We played a grocery store."

B: "You *what?!*"

T: "You heard me. A grocery store. Outside on a patio."

B: "Why?"

T: "Because a beverage was sponsoring the tour. And they were stocking it in that store. We drank the beverage from the stage and mentioned it in our banter and generally wanted to wrap dynamite around our heads and leave this cold, hard world."

B: "Was there a drug connection there?"

T: *(Pause.)* "Why do you ask?"

B: "Because you got fucked up on pills in Austin the year before, and the person you got them from was in Austin but lives near Dallas. And I've got the feeling he was one of the only two or three people on that patio listening to you."

T: "Yeah, he was there, but he didn't give me any pills!"

B: "I think he did."

T: "Fuck you. He gave me no pills."

B: "Why in the world should I believe you?"

T: "Because I'm telling the truth."

B: "You swore to God to Lisa that he gave you no pills."

T: "He didn't!"

B: "To *God!*"

T: "No!"

B: "A preacher's son doesn't swear to God, Tommy, especially if you're, you know, *lying.*"

Tommy stared hard at me. He swallowed deeply, probably still trying to get that pain pill down his gullet, then he looked away, and then he blinked hard, then he said goodbye, got up from the table and left me to write my story.

I pretty much know what happened after that to the present. He and Lisa went on to Austin and played four showcases over three days at the South by Southwest festival. They stayed at the kind of motel where the maid leaves a lump of crack on your pillow. There's nothing fun to write about being there in all the frolic, because they didn't frolic. Tommy stayed in his room watching television every moment when he wasn't downtown playing a show. I can understand that. Tommy's been in the thick of it at so many SXSWs that it means nothing to him anymore. He's 49. Been there, done that, got a lot of T-shirts.

Then they made the cozy 16-hour drive back to Nashville in one fell swoop on Thursday, a traditional purgatory involved with that festival. He and Lisa played Saturday night the 17th in North Carolina at the Balsam Mountain Inn with Marshall, and that was nice. Tommy was off drugs and hadn't had a drink since the night of the Station Inn. Then a week went by when Tommy just worked at his day job, watched a lot of television, contemplated his woes and didn't do a thing regarding writing this book.

He sang a song with the Long Players at the Mercy Lounge on Friday the 23rd. The Long Players play classic albums all the way through, with different lead singers on each tune. The album that night was Crosby, Stills, Nash and Young's Déjà Vu, and Tommy sang "Almost Cut My Hair" while dancing around brandishing a pair of pinking shears. Comic relief is what you call on Tommy for, and he accepts that—most of the time.

I love Tommy, he's a great guy most of the time. I love him and I worry about him. He's a talented man-child who could amount to so much more in this world than he's so far pulled off, if he would just call a halt to throwing so many stones in his own pathway. I hear he's still off the sauce, and that's good. I'm sure he's abusing his prescription Xanax as sure as I am that the sun will come up tomorrow morning. And, while I don't know if he's snorting any pharmaceuticals off tabletops, I'm pretty sure he's dreaming of the next time he can.

y'shua drops in

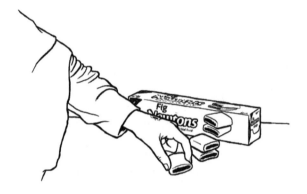

So Jesus walks up to somebody's house carrying a cross and three nails. Knock knock. A man comes to the door. Jesus says, "Can you put me up for the night?" OHHHH! Tough crowd. Tough crowd!

* * * * * *

The smell of popcorn, hot dogs and newly mown grass. Dew on the bleachers. Bugs underneath the floodlights. It is Friday, September 16, 1977. I'm 14 years old, towheaded with John Denver glasses, my hands in the pockets of my maroon jacket, pretending to watch the football game, standing next to the marching band up in the stands, pretending I'm playing an instrument with them, pretending I'm anybody other than who I am.

She's playing clarinet. Staci Ward. She's a freshman, with the biggest, roundest eyes, strawberry blonde hair underneath her maroon band helmet, smiling and talking to the clarinet player next to her, oblivious to my staring a hole in her. She's the cutest girl in the world. I'm obsessed with her, because that's what I do: I obsess about things. As Mom says, "Tom, when you get something in your head, there's no gettin' rid of it!" Apple, tree.

I've never talked to Staci. I never talk to any of the girls I'm ever in love with. There's no point. My being in puppy love with a girl automatically elevates her above my station. I want her, therefore I'll never have her. And by "want" I mean I'm 14 years old and I want to walk around the football field with her and drink Dr Pepper out of a waxy paper cup. I want all the other kids to see how cool I am, because I'm walking around with Staci Ward. I bet she lives in a big house with a two-car garage and a fridge with two doors. I bet she goes riding around in circles at the shopping center with friends, because that's what cool kids do. I want to be a cool kid.

The band plays "Low Rider" by War. I face the field. We score. The team. Not me.

* * * * * *

SCENE 1

The curtain rises to reveal a teenager's bedroom. It is the '70s. The walls are adorned with Kiss posters, interspersed with Aerosmith and Ted Nugent posters. TOMMY is seated on the edge of a messy, unmade bed, tapping at a typewriter on a wheeled tray. He is wearing jeans, a T-shirt and wire-framed glasses and has blond, '70s-style feathered hair. A small acoustic guitar leans against the bed next to him. There are stacks of paper all over the bed and all over the floor and on the wings of the tray the typewriter sits on. There are empty Mr. Pibb bottles on the floor, along with clothes and socks. A television is playing but TOMMY pays no attention to it. He is wearing headphones that are connected to a stereo system. A vinyl album is playing, silently it would seem to the audience, but apparently loudly in the phones, as TOMMY is bopping to the music as he types. Next to TOMMY on the bed is a high school yearbook opened to a certain page. Occasionally, amidst typing, TOMMY will gaze lovingly at a certain picture on that page in the yearbook, then sigh, and return to his typing.

The door to the bedroom opens. Enter Y'SHUA. He is dressed in the style of a 1st century Hebrew peasant. He wears a rough cloth, poor man's robe and sandals. There is a large bloodstain on the robe on his right side. He has bloody wounds on his hands and feet. He is dark-complexioned with long, kinky black hair and a full black beard.

TOMMY doesn't notice. His back is to the door. He keeps typing and bopping to the music in his headphones. Y'SHUA looks around at the Kiss posters, grinning, picks a Creem *magazine off the floor and leafs through it, chuckling. Then he sits down on the edge of the bed. The motion of his sitting makes TOMMY turn around.*

TOMMY: *(Startled.)* "Ahhhh!" *(Rips off the headphones.)* "Who the heck are you?"

Y'SHUA: *(Smiling, extending his hand.)* "I'm Y'shua, the guy you'll be writing about in 40 years."

TOMMY: *(Shaking hands.)* "Y'shua, huh?"

Y'SHUA: *(Smiles gently.)* "That's me!"

TOMMY: "Do I know you from school?"

Y'SHUA: "No, man! Think about it."

TOMMY: "I don't think about anything."

Y'SHUA: "Y'shua's an Aramaic name. It's the same root name we get Joshua from, and Jesus."

TOMMY: "You're Jesus?"

Y'SHUA: "In the flesh."

TOMMY: *(Rising and moving past Y'shua for the door.)* "I gotta go get Dad. He'll freak."

Y'SHUA grabs TOMMY by the sleeve.

Y'SHUA: "No, no. Let's not bother him. Sit back down."

TOMMY: "Well, okay."

Y'SHUA: "So how are you?"

TOMMY: "Terrible, man. There's nothing meaningful to do. Being 15 sucks so bad. Girls bum me out, I don't feel like I belong anywhere, so I just type and listen to music and try and figure out this guitar."

Y'SHUA: "That doesn't sound so bad."

TOMMY: "Yeah, but I'm depressed. All the time. I just can't shake it. People think I'm a real cut-up at school but that's just 'cause I'm scared to show them the real me because then they won't like me. Even if a lot of 'em don't like me to begin with."

Y'SHUA: *(Points up to a shelf.)* "Hey is that a Revised Standard Version Bible? Do you mind? Never seen one."

TOMMY: "You've never seen a Revised Standard Version Bible?"

Y'SHUA: "No. I got so upset at the Council of Nicea that I've tended to stay away from translations. Do you mind?"

TOMMY: "By all means. Go ahead."

Y'SHUA pulls the Bible off the shelf and starts leafing through the New Testament.

Y'SHUA: "Wrong! Wrong!" *(Rips out whole pages and throws them on the floor.)* "Wrong! Wrong! Wrong!"

TOMMY: "What are you doing?!"

Y'SHUA: "Nothing."

TOMMY: "But you're ripping pages out of my Bible!"

Y'SHUA: "Just pruning a little sectarian, Jew-bashing bullshit. You won't miss it. Hey, what are you listening to?"

TOMMY: "Ted Nugent. *Double Live Gonzo.*"

Y'SHUA: "Is it good?"

TOMMY: "Ted rocks."

Y'SHUA: "Mmmm-hmm. You got anything to munch on? I'm kinda hungry."

TOMMY: "We've got some ham from Sunday left."

Y'SHUA: "I'm Jewish, Tommy."

TOMMY: "You want some Doritos? Maybe a Reese's cup? A Mr. Pibb?"

Y'SHUA: "Do you even know what all that stuff does to your insides?"

TOMMY: "No."

Y'SHUA: "You got any figs?"

TOMMY: "Some Fig Newtons, I think."

Y'SHUA: "What are they like?"

TOMMY: "They're like Fig Newtons! I don't know. You want some?"

Y'SHUA: "Sure."

TOMMY: "Anything to drink? We have iced tea. You can turn it into anything you want."

Y'SHUA: "That'll be fine."

Exit TOMMY out bedroom door. Y'SHUA leans across the bed and browses more through the Bible. He begins breaking out in wild laughter, then reads some more and laughs loudly again and again. TOMMY enters, carrying a large plastic glass of iced tea and the box of Fig Newtons. He gives then to Y'SHUA.

TOMMY: "What's so funny?"

Y'SHUA: "Revelation!"

TOMMY: "So none of that's true?"

Y'SHUA: "Oh, what's true and what's not? It was true for him, that's what matters. Hey, is that *Charlie's Angels*?"

TOMMY: "That wasn't much of an answer."

Y'SHUA: "It was THE answer. Truth is wild, ephemeral stuff. Like, for instance . . " *(Flips through the pages of the Bible.)* "Here we are: 'It is easier for a camel to pass through the eye of a needle than for a rich man to enter the kingdom of heaven.' I said 'Rope, ROPE!' These idiots. You see, the Greek word for rope is *kamilos,* the Greek word for camel is *kamelos,* and so there you go. Some 6th century monk translator was tired and misspelled. And now everybody quotes me about passing camels through the eyes of needles! BUT, all that considered, the intended message remains the same. These Fig Newtons aren't bad." *(Y'SHUA takes a sip of tea and recoils from the glass.)* "Damn, how much sugar do you people put in your iced tea?"

TOMMY: "What was it like back then?"

Y'SHUA: "What do you mean?"

TOMMY: "I mean, doing all those miracles, the Transfiguration, walking on the water, all that? What was it like?"

Y'SHUA: "It was fun." *(Y'SHUA fiddles with the stereo, pulls out the headphone jack; music fills the room.)* "This rocks. What's that song?"

TOMMY: "It's called 'Yank Me, Crank Me, But Don't Wake Up and Thank Me.' Please, tell me things. Tell me about the Passion!"

Y'SUA: "I don't remember much."

TOMMY: "You don't *remember much?* It's the single most important weekend in Christendom. We base our whole belief and the health of our souls on how you died for us that weekend! And now you tell me you don't remember!"

Y'SHUA: "We drank a lot of wine that weekend."

TOMMY: "Did you really change water into wine?"

Y'SHUA: "Please. It's all symbolism. The water represents the old Jerusalem. The wine cask represents the Temple. The new wine represents me. Bada bing."

TOMMY: "But what about when you fed five thousand people on three baskets of fish? Or was it three thousand people and five baskets of fish? I never can remember."

Y'SHUA: "That represents how all who come to worship will be satisfied and that there's enough of me to go around. You know, it's a Gospel, not a history. It was a common effect of Gospels that all the

symbolism made sense to a 1st century Jew, and they *knew* some parts
of the Gospels were written with a nod and a wink. Not too literally."

TOMMY: "But all the people you raised from the dead . . ."

Y'SHUA: "Some get better, some don't. The life of a shaman . . ."

TOMMY: "I'm sorry but I just HAVE to go tell this to Dad."

Y'SHUA: "NO!"

TOMMY: "My Dad's been preaching about you all his life. He loves
you more than anything. You're his whole world. Mom's, too. They'll
be thrilled to meet you. Dad's watching *Barnaby Jones* right now, he
likes Buddy Ebsen, but I'm sure he'd hit mute to meet you. Mom's
probably watching it, too. You can meet them both."

Y'SHUA: "After two thousand years, I've learned—just let people see
me how they want to. And let's not interrupt a Quinn Martin Production
just to shatter a sweet couple's illusions."

TOMMY: "Well, why are you here talking to me?"

Y'SHUA: "Because I want you to know things will all be better someday. The adolescence of a budding comic is very hard. High school's
tough. And you're going to be praying to me and wanting things to be
better and they're not going to get better for a long while, and you're
going to question my existence and you'll just stop praying to me after
a while. For those who don't question me, let 'em live! Let 'em think I
rose out of a grave and made dead birds fly and could cut a deck of cards
with one hand and what all else. It doesn't matter."

TOMMY: "But if I don't believe that you can die on a cross and
rise from the dead after three days of decomposition, won't that
mean I'm going to fry like a slice of country ham in a lake of fire for
eternity?"

Y'SHUA: "Why don't you just let me worry about that? So what are
you writing here?"

TOMMY: "It's a Robin Hood parody called 'Robin Who?'"

Y'SHUA: "Most kids your age haven't written a book. You should be proud."

TOMMY: "Yeah, but it just makes the other kids think I'm weirder than they already do. It's not like being able to put the orange bouncy ball though a hoop. Or kick a football between goalposts. THAT's what these people around here value. And it sure hasn't made Staci Ward like me."

Y'SHUA: "She's never going to like you."

TOMMY: "Thank you."

Y'SHUA: The truth will set you free. Right after it pisses you off." *(Reading.)* "Heh, heh! This is funny! You're not bad for a high school geek. Listen, I gotta go. Remember what we talked about."

TOMMY: "What, dashing a few illusions?"

Y'SHUA: "Life is an illusion. Truth is an illusion. Beauty, grace, mental health, ALL illusions! You're going to get a job as the church janitor before long, and you're going to go off the deep end depression-wise. You're going to be vacuuming the rug up and down between pews and you'll be crying and you'll howl in the empty church sanctuary as you look up at that big cross on the wall.

"And by the way, that cross. I don't like the whole cross thing at *all!* Do Irish Jack Kennedy fans dangle little Mannlicher-Carcano scope rifles around their necks? If people would think for half a second they'd realize why I haven't come back yet. The last thing I ever want to see again is a cross!"

TOMMY: "But you . . ."

Y'SHUA: "Died for your sins?"

TOMMY: "Right! I . . . have trouble with that one."

Y'SHUA: "That's okay. It's okay to doubt, you know. Life's rough. Hey, thanks for the Fig Newtons. Can I take a few?"

TOMMY: "Take the box. They were in the back of the cabinet. Nobody knew we had them, anyway."

Y'SHUA: "The box is convenient. No pockets in this robe."

TOMMY: "Nice to meet you, Y'shua."

Y'SHUA: "You too, Tommy. Just don't intentionally hurt anybody else, try to make at least one person smile every day, don't lie, don't scheme, pray, and be nice and considerate. Those are the cards you play for a life with which I will be well pleased."

TOMMY: "Thou art Jesus the Christ! The Messiah. I give you praise and glory."

Y'SHUA: "Right. Take it easy."

Exit Y'SHUA.

TOMMY takes a swig of Mr. Pibb, cranks the stereo without the head-phones so the music is blaring loudly in the room. He resumes typing.

Enter DAD. He wears Sunday pants with suspenders, a Sunday shirt with a glasses case in the front pocket. He wears wire-frame glasses and a frown.

DAD: "Turn that crap down!"

TOMMY turns down the stereo, but continues typing with his back to DAD.

DAD: "Who was just here?"

TOMMY: "Nobody."

DAD: "I thought I heard somebody back here."

TOMMY: *(Typing blithely away.)* "Nope."

Exit DAD.

Re-enter DAD.

DAD: "Boy?"

TOMMY: "What?"

DAD: "Where are the Fig Newtons?"

TOMMY: "I have no idea."

The curtain falls.

back and forth bad, up and down good

Saturday, May 19, 2012

Chattanooga, Tennessee. Played Charles and Myrtle's Coffeehouse at the Unitarian church tonight. It was actually a pretty good turnout, which means maybe as many as 25 people. That's a good gig for me.

They were polite acoustic music lovers. I was able to play the quiet songs on a canvas of silence, which was nice for a change, and they laughed at the jokes, more or less. I have a friend, Travis, who's a big fan and sings harmony from his seat whenever I play Chattanooga. It's always a little eerie, but nice, to hear a harmony vocal caressing my melody from across the room. Doesn't bother me if people want to do that, so long as they can sing. At least they're listening. Merch sales were good. I might be able to buy a new box of *Cheese Chronicles* after this gig. We'll see.

I'm sleeping over at the church because I'm singing during the service tomorrow, which I'm informed is a real loose affair (and I'm guessing hippie-fied). Here I am, alone, on a freshly made bed in the basement of a church, in my comfy sleep clothes, waiting for a psycho to kick out one of the ground-level windows and stab me to death. All this for forty extra bucks to be had for singing at the service—and whatever merch I can sell to the congregation. By the way, I can sing anything I want in the morning, they told me. I can sing "Camping on Acid" if I want to. They once had an entire service dedicated to the spiritual journey of Jimmy Buffett, closing the morning out with "Margaritaville."

* * * * * *

I grew up in a loving home and it took me way too long to appreciate that. It's not like Mom was depressed or Dad inert *all the time.* We had good Christmases with cool toys. We had an aluminum tree with red and blue balls for ornaments. Dad set up a spinning color wheel shining different color lights onto our reflective tree. We would turn off the living room lights and watch it. We did things. In Paducah we went to Noble Park and swam, we went weekends to Kentucky Lake, borrowed a cottage from a parishioner, fished and swam.

Mom had a memory of Dad getting grumpy setting up a portable charcoal grill down by the dock, and he was having a difficult time doing it, and was getting more volatile and taking it all out on us, in a voice loud enough to be heard by other people nearby who gave us weird looks. I don't remember that one. You can't remember all of them when you're three or four years old. But Mom was mortified.

But then again I remember cuddling on the couch with Dad while he read me the funny papers. This is all stuff I remember after we moved to West Paducah in 1966, when I was three going on four.

* * * * * *

Sunday, May 20, 2012

Nathan and I watched the *Rush: Beyond the Lighted Stage* documentary DVD tonight. Rush is a Canadian rock trio, in case you've been under a rock the last 35 years. They specialize in polyrhythmic hard rock that is impossible to dance to, with loquacious, dictionary-breath lyrics that are unintentionally hilarious. I used to hate them but I like them now. Hell, it's Rush.

Watching the documentary took me back to senior year of high school, 1979, in my bedroom pecking on the typewriter, working on a book, listening to a borrowed copy of *Permanent Waves.* I remember reading the lyrics on the album sleeve and chuckling.

> *"One likes to believe in the freedom of music! But glittering prizes and endless compromises, shatter the illusion of integrity, yeah!"*

Oh, yes, "One likes!" he sings, "one likes!" Yes, one must like, mustn't one! Harrumph! But the real kicker was *". . . shatter the illusion of integrity, yeah!"* It's like somebody said, Hey, make that lyric a little more rock 'n' roll: put a "yeah!" in there! *". . . shatter the illusion of integrity, YEAH!"* Alright! Now THAT'S rock 'n' roll!

So Rush didn't excite me much then. I like them now, though. A rule in rock 'n' roll is that if you last long enough, you'll be cool. That applies to all acts except Mike Love's version of the Beach Boys.

* * * * * *

I wrote two books in high school: *The Secrets of Yuk* and *Yuk II.* They were collections of short stories and vignettes, and while it was sophomoric doggerel, it was well-written doggerel for a kid in high school. I would take the only copies to school and shove them in people's faces. Some loved it, actually, some kids read half a page and handed it back saying, "Womack, you're just dumb."

Only one copy of each book has ever existed, first-generation typewritten pages bound together with staples, glue and manila folder fronts, backs and spines. You'll never read them. I know they're in the house but I don't know where. I wish I knew where they were just so I could secure them and ensure no one would ever see them should I get hit by a bus. Although I'm actually still proud of one of my short stories, "The Bionic Vampire," the derring-do tales of Count Spatula. I was learning my craft, like budding comics do. Through hard work we improve over time.

* * * * * *

I had the time to write two whole books in high school because I didn't know how to masturbate. I was 16 with zits, pecking at a typewriter and out of my goddam mind. I wouldn't learn how to jack off until I was 19, and even then it was a female who demonstrated it on me in the front seat of a car. (Bless you, dear. You opened up a whole new world.)

It was around the time of that Rush album in senior year that I would ride around in Mike Howard's car all over town on Friday nights, while he tried to talk me out of my depression. I was always going moony over some girl, and feeling like life wasn't complete without her, and she wouldn't have anything to do with me, moan, sob, sniffle. I would whine and Mike would counsel.

He was dropping me off at home late one Friday night and I had been mentioning that I wished I knew how to masturbate. I knew there was something that *could be done,* I just didn't know how you actually *did* it!

I was standing outside the open passenger car door. Mike leaned over and with his right hand made a ring with his thumb and forefinger. "You see this?" he said, "Do your hand like this, put it over your dick and move it back and forth."

"Uh, okay." I said. "Later."

I went in the house, into my bedroom, took off my jeans and my sweater, got into bed in my skivvies and my T-shirt, reached inside to my ever-present erection, made a ring out of my thumb and forefinger, slipped it over my perky penis, and moved it back and forth, like a gear-shift. Forward toward my balls, backward to my belly button, forward to my balls, backward to my belly button. Over and over. Perhaps if Mike had said "up and down" instead of "back and forth," I would have hopped on the clue bus. As it was, I did the gearshift for a bit, didn't get what the fuss was about, put my dick back in its cage, flipped out the light and went to sleep.

17

it was a great gig up to a point!

It's been a fantastic Memorial Day weekend of great music, great friends and great times. Friday, I played Hippie Jack's festival, had a great time and went to jail on a DUI, then I had another great gig Saturday afternoon at the Flatrock Festival here in town.

The Jammin' at Hippie Jack's festival is held on Hippie Jack Stoddart's farm in Crawford, Tennessee, about 100 miles east of Nashville, where the hills start to become mountains. Hippie's place is in a gorgeous valley surrounded by steep, forested ridges. It wasn't as oppressively hot as we'd been steeling ourselves for; as a matter of fact, inside the tent where the shows and the audience were, it was darn comfortable. All over the valley, tents were everywhere, the people staying there the whole weekend—craft and concession tents were up, too.

Hippie Jack is a great and interesting guy. In the late '60s/early '70s, he helped found The Farm on these very grounds. It was one of the original "get back to the land" hippie communes. A bus full of hippies in San Francisco hopped into a bus like the Merry Pranksters and came all the way to Tennessee, to get back to the land, man. Jessica Kimbrough, Will's wife, grew up there.

But that was then and this is now. His farm is not the commune it was then, but it is still the home of Jack's family, going down to the grandkids. And they all team up to produce the very successful *Jammin' at Hippie Jack's* television show, an hourlong musical series that is run on 300-ish public television stations. I've done that show before, Will and I as a duet, and it was a gas.

Lisa and I played along with Marshall Chapman in her set and that went really well. Dan and Justin from my band backed up Sam Lewis, who was incredible, my major discovery of the festival. And then we had a bang-up show. It really rocked.

Then the next day, Saturday afternoon, my band was joined by a horn section and Michael Webb on keyboards, and we did the Flatrock Festival in Coleman Park, not two miles from my house. This day, it *was* oppressively hot. There was a tent with tables off to our left, and some people were there listening to us, but not a lot of action on the grass right in front of us. We all played well, though I'll confess to being a little tired. Lisa did a set with my band and then we did my set. Convenient, that. It was fun, but steamy sweaty. Not good rock 'n' roll sweaty—more like verge of heatstroke sweaty.

I did the shows, loaded my gear into the van, went home, took off all my sweat-drenched clothes and rubbed myself down with a wet rag from head to toe, then dried myself off and put on entirely new dry clothes, all the while giving thanks to God for that wonderful fellow who invented air conditioning. Then I flopped out on the bed, ordered Chinese, and fell asleep waiting for it to arrive, for I was weary. I hadn't gotten a lot of quality sleep the night before.

Oh, yeah, the DUI.

We had been getting warnings at Hippie's all afternoon that the Overton County Sheriff's Department was staking out the exit off the dirt road leaving Hippie's compound, right across the county line. Hippie and his wife both implored us. "We have couches and sleeping bags aplenty. You don't have to leave tonight." We heard it and heard it. When someone asks, "Are you okay to drive?" you reply, "Look, I'm a musician." And that's supposed to be 'nuff said.

Hey, it works. It's worked for years. I've been driving smashed for 15 records now. I've come home so many times seeing two streetlights for every one that was really there. And awakened so many mornings cringing over having escaped the Reaper one more time, and, God be praised, not hurting anyone else. With all the warnings, I wasn't too concerned. Hell, that was par for my course! Just as we were pulling out to leave, Hippie came up to my van and gave me a last hug and a kiss on the cheek and asked for sure if we didn't want to stay the night.

I'd been 100 percent sober before and during the shows I'd done, both sitting in with Marshall and doing my own bit. Chris, Marshall's husband, had even complimented me on how clear-eyed and alert I was, and how I was not twitching and blinking so much, he thinking no doubt that I was still in "the program" when I hadn't been to a meeting in months, and was drinking on the quiet a bit too.

But after my show that evening, with the adrenaline and good feeling and the one .5 mg Xanax I'd scored, and whatever else kind of excuse I can hang it on, I wanted a drink.

At these festivals there are always sweetheart people approaching who will get you whatever you want. I found one of those people just at the same time he found me, and I asked for a discreet drink of whiskey. Ten minutes later I was presented a plastic cup with maybe an inch and a half of Wild Turkey in it. I'd say there were two healthy shots in that glass, and I drank it discreetly next to the monitor soundboard offstage, watching the Wild Ponies, and then I felt great and went off to socialize.

It was such a good time. So many lovely people, hippies and semi-straights mixing together, Grayson Capps sounding great onstage, me having a great conversation with Sam Lewis, and then getting everything together to leave, loading up the equipment, getting the merch from the merch tent, settling up for the sales, etc.

Up by the van, I was thinking about what a great day it had been. I took two hits of pot that was being passed around. Yes, I felt good, and as we pulled out, after that one last (pleading) goodbye from Hippie, I felt completely *compos mentis*. The fucked-up guy is always the last to know. I was putting on enough of a sober-acting front to keep my band comfortable and unworried. That's how I was thinking.

The first five miles of the drive home were great. It's a dangerous mountain road that winds around and has drop-offs you don't want to mess with, and I navigated it all nimbly like any experienced musician with a drinking problem could. Then we came to the paved road and had a nice mile stretch of driving to the highway intersection that would take us to the interstate. And there they were.

There were at least three sheriffs' cruisers, all with their blue lights twirling prettily, with officers standing in the middle of the road with flashlights. Of course I was brought to a stop.

He was Officer Jonathan Stout. I had socks older than Officer Stout. But the shoe wasn't on the aged foot this evening.

"How are you, sir?"

"Fine, officer, how are you?" I was chomping on a piece of gum like I was trying to kill it.

"Have you been drinking this evening sir?"

"Nnnno."

"Sir," he monotoned, "your eyes tell a different story; they're red and glassy. Would you step out of the vehicle, please?"

Officer Stout put me through the stupid human tricks. His diction was like the neighbor on *King of the Hill* who speaks complete gibberish. I kept having to ask him to repeat his instructions on each next gymnastic pattern he wanted me to perform. I was shaking. Things were really sinking in to me now. "Just relax, Mr. Womack. Don't be nervous." *(Jes er lax misser walmack, don b'narviss!)* Don't be nervous? Are you fucking kidding me?

I failed every one of the tricks, including a couple I couldn't have done sober. He made me follow a penlight with my eyes. He made me throw my head back and count 30 seconds aloud. I don't know if I took 30 seconds or five minutes. It was a pristine rendition of 30 seconds to me, at the time.

It seemed, I thought optimistically, that I was maybe doing borderline well enough that young Officer Stout was having to keep pulling out trick after trick to perform, hoping I'd screw up enough for him to finally bag his quarry. It worked.

"Mr. Womack, please put your hands behind your back." *(Msrromack pleazpucherands hindjerback.)* And with cuffs snapped on for the first time in my life, I was put in the back seat of a police car. After all these years, my chickens had come home to roost, and shit on my head.

Once I was in the back of the squad car, a curious calm came over me. I was nervous as hell doing the stupid human tricks, but now that was over, and I was caught, and I was cuffed, and I was in the back seat. For some reason, I was now serene. I told myself, remember this, Tommy, remember all of it. This is *just what the book needs right now.*

I had a lot of time to think while I watched them *pull the whole band out of the van* and put them through the same paces. As it turned out, Mark passed a Breathalyzer and he drove them all home, but I wouldn't know that for hours. My cellphone was in the van. I would have no contact with any of them until the next day. I would have no idea what happened to them or what any of them might have been doing on my behalf. I was Captain Clueless. I was as worried for them as for myself. For a brief moment, at least.

Funny how they didn't Breathalyzer me, but I guess the pot changes everything. I got the feeling that once I'd told him I'd smoked marijuana, I may as well have told him I'd just drunk blood from an infant's skull. I agreed to a blood test because they explained to me that if I refused the test and lost my case in court, I could lose my license for a year. So that's the first place they took me, the nearest ER, which wasn't near at all.

I knew the drill, shut the fuck up, speak when spoken to and throw "Sir" in every other word. But when Stout and his partner (who was younger than my jeans) sat down in the front seats, they took no notice of me. I was no more than a shot-dead four-point buck bagged and thrown into the truck bed. I got my first very faint inkling about where the animosity starts between the outlaws and the authorities, because if the arrest had been bullshit—which it wasn't—and I had been talked to roughly—which I hadn't—then I would by then have been just pissed off enough to be on O.J.'s jury. They put on some music. Christian pop. That gave me another clue as to whom I was dealing with.

Like a bat out of hell we barreled down winding highways, blew through little towns, past farmland, and this Wally Cleaver with a badge had that squad cruiser going 70-plus at every opportunity, slowing down to 55 in the speed-trap towns where the posted limit is 35 mph. All the while they listened to that damn Christian pop. I was in the back seat with my painful cuffed hands behind my back, being pummeled by *"Our God is an awesome God! I'm so happy He's my God! I'm so fucking happy!!!! La la la!!!"*

After a small eternity we pulled up to a hospital emergency room, me convinced I could have driven us there more safely in my condition than Wally Cleaver did in his. They let me out of the car and Stout escorted me to the front door of the emergency room. "So you've smoked a serious amount of marijuana tonight, Mr. Womack?"

"I had two tokes, sir," I replied quietly. All my mutterings were quiet now. Quiet and fawning. "So in other words you smoked a serious amount," he replied. Yes, officer, I said to myself, I have smoked a serious amount, *IN YOUR FUCKING WORLD!* Your world where your God is an Awesome God, in 4/4 time, with a digital piano and a choir through Autotune and a really really happy singer. THAT'S your world, baby-face!

At the registration desk, a receptionist took my information and Officer Stout, who appeared to maybe like me by now, undid my cuffs. "Here," he said, "we can let you put your hands in front. You're not giving me any problems." I was grateful. The cuffs felt much better in front than in back. I was taken into a lab room and my blood was drawn. It was bagged up to be taken off to a state analysis lab and I'm wondering to myself what in holy hell will they be finding in there. I was rewinding tapes in my memory bank trying to recall what I'd put in my system and how recently it may have been. I might as well have asked myself to name the 10 most recent popes.

"Mr. Womack," Officer Stout said *(Mssromack),* "I hope this is a lesson for you," thus triggering a silent "fuck you" in my brain. "Yes, sir," I said. "Absolutely, sir. Thank you, sir."

And then we were back in the squad car; much more comfortably for me with my cuffed hands in my lap! And off Wally Cleaver screamed for another long, rubber-burning carom through bumfuck, Overton County. After a few hairpin turns and some pedal-stomping on the straightways, we pulled up to the sheriff's office, and the Overton County jail, my new home away from home. There was a little handoff between Officer Stout and the jailer, who was even younger than the cops. The fucking Mickey Mouse Club was handling my whole collar.

I was actually scared to be seeing Officer Stout go. I'd grown to be dependent on his oddly reassuring garbled affirmations. I asked him what I could expect and he told me I would be there at least four hours or maybe until morning, and then I could "bond out," and he said that as if I knew what anything meant. He had no words of wisdom past that. Although he did say, "With any luck, you'll make it to your show tomorrow."

Just as he left he again said, "Mr. Womack, I hope you learn something from this." "Yes, sir." "You may lose your job over this," he felt the need to add. "Yes, sir." He didn't need to say that but I suppose it was a good thing to think about. "Now, these people will take good care of you. Good luck, Mr. Womack." *(G'luck msromack.)* "Thank you, sir."

The jailer looked like he was 18 years old. As he took my cuffs off, he asked me, "You're not going to give me any trouble, are you?" "No, sir," I said. I was calling an 18-year-old bumpkin "sir."

I surrendered my wallet, the contents of my pockets, 21 guitar picks (they counted them), my shoes and my belt, and I was put in an oddly shaped, small, triangular room with six other fellows. Two of them were out cold on the floor, lying on thin mats with thin blankets over them. Another was asleep up on a bench; the other three, a bearded guy, a small, wiry guy and a mutant with no top teeth, were sitting or standing and holding court. I sat down cross-legged on the floor against one wall, about two feet from the stainless steel toilet with no fold-up seat. *(The better not to rip off and bash you over the head with, my dear!)*

"Whatcha here for? DUI?" asked the bearded guy.

"Yeah," I sighed, "DUI."

Now I've watched a lot of *Lockup* marathons. I am very intrigued by prison life, and now here I was getting a taste from inside the machine. I sat there on the floor against the wall and it occurred to me that

I still had a pretty nice Jack and weed buzz. I was glad to have it, even though if I hadn't had it I wouldn't have been there.

The three wakeful ones were professional inmates, and boy, did they like to talk. They were only in the drunk tank while their own cells were being refurbished (or torn apart) or having all the blood mopped up or who the fuck knows. The wiry one was in for seven months, and it didn't seem to bother him one bit. The bearded guy mentioned that he was 28 and had been in and out of seven jails and two prisons in the last eight years, and he didn't seem to be bothered about it, either. They were talking about how GOOD it is to be in a jail where you get a cup of coffee five times a week. As for the mutant, he spoke nonstop and I could catch only a third of what he said, and apparently the others didn't understand him much better. As I type this, I know those three guys are still there, quipping back and forth about how this jail is better than that jail, or not as good as that other one.

Wiry guy asked me why I was in this neck of the woods. "You out at that festival?" "Yes," I said (I was speaking only if spoken to), "I was the seven o'clock entertainment." "Well," wiry guy barked, "I wish I had the buzz you got right now!" And they all laughed. I guess I was pretty obvious. Like I said, you're always the last to know.

Mutant stationed himself at the door, always looking out through the metal-infused glass at the central hub where two lady jailers, the bumpkin and two trustees were. Mutant wanted to be a trustee, and the guy sleeping on the bench roused himself long enough to say, "You could do it. You're a good talker."

The guys started shouting through the door. "We need mats! And one for the new guy, too!" First lesson. In jail, if you need anything, you bang on the wire-mesh window in the door and you brusquely express your need, and the staff will take their sweet time accommodating you because they're in charge and it's going to stay that way.

Eventually we got mats, and I wedged mine in between the two mummies on the floor, young guys more passed out than asleep, I suspected. I tried to doze, and nearly succeeded. Nearly. The guys all seemed blessedly innocuous enough; anal rape didn't seem to be on the agenda, but I was uncomfortable sleeping.

Around 1:30 a.m. I was roused and summoned outside to the counter, where I was commanded to stand in a red-painted square on the floor. Bumpkin asked, "Mr. Womack, do you feel well enough now to be booked?"

"Yes, sir." I was terrified. I thought I'd already *been* booked. I'd been there two hours by now. What do you mean "booked"? The thought flashed through me. Does that mean I get moved into the back with all the lifers and knifers? Does that mean I'm here for two weeks? Bumpkin assured me that we were just going through the registration process to have me in the system to show that I was ever there. He sat down at the computer and for the next 20, maybe 30 minutes attempted to book me into the computer system. Bumpkin was not only young and inexperienced. If you put his brains in a bird, it would fly backwards. He pecked at the keyboard slowly, and kept screwing up, kept asking the two ladies for help, wondering what info to put in what fields. Once he hollered, "Linda, where do I type in his age?" Linda walked over and pointed, "Right there where it says 'age.'" He kept stopping and having to start over. He had trouble getting documents to print. He took five minutes at the copier trying to make front and back copies of my driver's license. He took an extensive medical history, and when it got to the words "antidepressants" and "anxiety" I had to spell them out for him. A couple of times, the trustees even had to coach him on his spelling. I had to sign my name about six times on documents, and then he had to print out new ones for half of them because he'd asked me to sign on the wrong line and we had to start over. I signed my name a lot.

By the time he got through the agonizing process 30 minutes had passed and my skinny feet with high arches were killing me from standing in that red square on the cement floor. He took me over to the wall with the height marks on it and took my mug shots, and then took me to the electronic fingerprinting machine, which, like everything else, didn't go smoothly. And somewhere around this point, he professed, "Well, Mr. Womack, I hope this is a lesson to you."

"Yes, sir." *(Fuck you toddler!)*

"'Cause this is no place you want to be," he said, like a redneck sage.

"Yes, sir." *(Blow me.)*

He instructed me to pick out a blanket from one of the shelves and pick out a pair of flip-flops. They felt heavenly on my feet even if they didn't fit at all.

Next was the agonizing process of choosing one of the bail-bondsman services printed on the wall next to the phone on the wall. The phone had a very short cord *(The better not to strangle you with, my dear!)*. You had to lean almost to the phone itself to hold it to your ear. A trustee helped me out with it. He was a big, very muscular guy with tattoos over all his exposed body. He was smiling and very nice to me, wanting to help me out. "Hell," he said, "I wanna help anybody wanting to get the fuck out of this place." He had a winning smile but something in his eyes said he liked to beat the fuck out of people too. I learned later back in the holding cell that I had diagnosed him exactly right. He'd just recently beaten up his cellie. And this guy was a trustee, hanging out front with the staff and shooting the shit!

Then back I went to the cell, where we'd had a few new arrivals, and I lay back down on my mat, taking notice that someone had taken mine and replaced it with a threadbare one. OK, so *that's* how it's going to be. I didn't pursue the matter. I tried to use the toilet, which was very difficult. I have bashful kidneys and I was trying to pee with nine other people in a seven-by-ten holding room, which meant standing there for two minutes before anything came out.

Then I settled down again between the two mummies, and believe it or not, I slept. Not for very long at any one time, but I did sleep. Until 6 a.m., when the lights came on full blast. The room went from one light bulb that had always been on to enough fluorescent light to film *Citizen Kane*. "Chow time!" I had no interest in chow, but boy, the bearded bubba did. He ate my chow and the mummies' chow. Then he said, "Goddam, I'm stuffed. Maybe today I'll shit!" Well, buddy, I hope you do!

The next thing I knew, I heard my name being said on the other side of the door. I got up and stumbled in my ill-fitting flip-flops and went to the door window, trying to see through the wire mesh in the glass. Across the staff counter there was another window, and behind it a window showing a sunny morning. And there at the window was Beth, her eyes as beautiful as the night we met. She winked at me and gave me a thumbs-up, then ran her hands across her head in a hint for me to smooth down my hair, which was greasy and anarchic.

They let me out of the cell and I stood in the red square, with Beth around the corner at the counter speaking to one of the jailers. From there things went fast. Before long I had my belt and my shoes and my wallet back. Then I was outside in a garage area where Beth and I met with Kim, our nice bail-bonds lady, and we did all her paperwork, Beth filling out the forms in her faultless handwriting while I was still really wishing I had that buzz that got me here. It was gone, and it didn't even say goodbye.

Then we were in the car for the 70-minute drive home. When we got home I dozed until gig time. Then I did the gig, came home and ordered Chinese, fell asleep, woke up, ate the Chinese, and fell back asleep for 14 hours. That bed had never felt better.

Then it was Sunday, and I jammed with Nathan, and played chess with him, shot my Monday Morning Cup of Coffee video blog I do, and then I wrote all this down, knowing as I was doing it that all this hadn't sunk in yet. I have a court date June 5. I've left a voicemail for an old fraternity brother who's a lawyer now. Someday soon I'll freak out about all this, but right now I'm planed on Xanax again. Tomorrow's another day, but it could be a really fucked-up day. I needed a wake-up call, and I'm awake now, not *wide* awake, but maybe that'll come. Maybe.

18

ch-ch-changes

It is a cold December Saturday night in 1979. I'm 16 years old, still obsessed with Staci Ward. I am seeing a counselor. I have my driver's license, the family four-door Gran Torino, and I'm driving around in Staci's neighborhood. It's nicer than mine. I figured it would be. All my unrequited love objects have lived in better neighborhoods than mine. With better lives and happy homes.

She knows I have a crush on her. I even called her once. It was the most brutal torture I've ever laid on myself. All the awkward pauses! I had so much to say and no tongue for it. She had nothing to say at all. It ended quickly. And I'll hate talking on phones for the rest of my life.

My crush on her is common knowledge at school. I've been obvious and mentioned it to too many people. I was either trying out comedy routines on people or rhapsodizing over Staci Ward. Word on the street is she thinks I'm crazy, like really wacked-out. And I apparently gross her the fuck out, too! Could be the nose-picking, the twitching, the bad breath I'm beginning to think I might have.

I pull over to the curb on the opposite side of the street and just stare at her house, bucking for a temporary restraining order. I play WLS-AM from Chicago on the car radio, and "Fire" by the Pointer Sisters is crackling through. I just stare at her house, my eyes tallying every window. Maybe she's behind one of those right now, or maybe she's out on the town with her friends who all have better lives than I do.

I put the Torino in park across from her house, the engine running and the heater on, WLS crackling. I undo my belt, pull my pants down to my knees, I stick my forefinger up my butt as far as it will go and I wiggle it around. With my finger covered with shit like a pen, I write TW & SW 4 EVER on the inside of the windshield with my own shit. Okay, I don't really do this, but I'm thinking maybe someday I'll write a book about all this, and maybe Staci will read it, and then I can GROSS HER THE FUCK OUT ONE MORE TIME!!!

* * * * * *

February 7, 2007

I Almost Died

I almost died, I almost died
The Lord or the devil nearly had my hide
Everything ground to a halt inside
God in Heaven I almost died

I was walking down 21st Avenue South
Camel Light sticking out the front of my mouth
It might have been blow
It might have been meth
All I know is I was starving to death
Had a ninety-dollar habit every week or so
Coffee and cigs let my tank run low

I almost died, I almost died
The Lord or the devil nearly had my hide
Everything ground to a halt inside
God in Heaven I almost died

I was so damn hungry I could swallow my knees
What I had left on me wouldn't make a dog sneeze
I was skiing downhill off a two-day run
You do it and you do it 'til it's gone, then you're done
It might have been meth
It might have been blow
These days honey you just don't know

I almost died, I almost died
The Lord or the devil nearly had my hide
Everything ground to a halt inside
God in Heaven I almost died

I was holding my stomach at the coffee shack
I blinked once good and I was on my back
Laid in the manger of an ambulance
They were pulling up my shirt and pulling down my pants
Slapping little stickers all over me
Attaching little wires for an EKG
Saying please be honest buddy what are you on?
You won't get in trouble, just your heart was gone
Then it took off running like a mad greyhound
Took two shots of Ativan to bring it back down
Hell they emptied my pockets and found my shit
There was no point lying so I copped to it
Somebody asked me what year this was
And I answered wrong like a dead man does

I almost died, I almost died
The Lord or the devil nearly had my hide
Everything ground to a halt inside
God in Heaven I almost died

I think about now how I almost died
How my son doesn't know how his momma cried
Did it scare me to death, yes I believe so
Did it make me stop, hell no

I almost died, I almost died
The Lord or the devil nearly had my hide
Everything ground to a halt inside
God in Heaven I almost died

* * * * * *

That song happened exactly as it is described. I cracked a vertebra
falling flat on my back in the Hillsboro Village Shell station when . . .
apparently . . . my heart stopped. As you can tell from the song the ambulance personnel pulled me back into my mortal coil. So the ER gave
me a scrip for Lortabs. (That was so sweet of them. Folks are so nice.)

I recovered well enough to play a gig in Evansville, Indiana, on Saturday. I came back home and the next day I enlisted Nathan, nine years old, to help me lick and stamp all the envelopes full of CDs to send the radio stations. He so enjoyed doing something with his daddy that he hugged me when we were done. I thought long and hard after that (still do) about how I nearly robbed this beautiful boy of his dad forever. It put my heart in my mouth and it happens, to this day, every time I think of it. To think I came that close.

Two weeks after that incident, my new record, *There, I Said It!*, was released, I was the cover story of the *Nashville Scene,* my face in the front of newsstands all over town, I had a great release concert, for a few days there I was toast of the town—and nobody knew a thing.

* * * * * *

We moved to Madisonville from West Paducah on November 22, 1968. I had just turned six two days before. We had found our new house, at 756 Plainview Drive, Madisonville, Kentucky, the Best Town on Earth *(kiss my aeeiss)*, and it wouldn't be long before I was in for a rude shock.

In West Paducah we lived on a highway corner out in the sticks. There were no other kids to play with. And I grew quite comfortable inventing playmates in my head. I had my G.I. Joes and staged mock battles. Mom safety-pinned a towel to my back for a cape and I pretended to be Batman. I was quite happy growing up alone those years. I saw kids on Sunday morning when everybody came to church, and that would be it. And of course I saw my siblings Jerry and Sissie (my name for Rhena) when they came home from school. But I had a lot of solitary fun out in the yard when Mom was tired and lying down. I never felt deprived or lonely. Madisonville was a whole different scene. A decidedly new phase of life.

Plainview Drive was a dead-end quarter-mile-long stick of pavement off Princeton Pike on the outskirts of town. There were 12 one-car-garage brick houses on one side and 13 on the other. A larger subdivision was barely peeking over a ridge to the east, but there were no connecting streets, just fields all around. If your only way to get around was a bicycle you couldn't take on the highway, and you lived on Plainview Drive, it was your whole world.

With about 20 sets of parents among 25 houses, it was a young population explosion on that street. There were kids older than me, younger than me. The street was abuzz with bicycle traffic, tricycles, Big Wheel traffic, mini-bikes, Wiffle-ball games in the middle of the road, anything that could be thought of to amuse kids and make drivers very careful.

It was the small-town coal miners' subdivision version of a tough neighborhood. Arguments and fistfights weren't uncommon. You had to earn your way in. You had to learn how to thrust and parry, and I had no experience with it. Jerry and Rhena hadn't had *that* much experience, either, and we all had different ways of dealing with it.

That first day we were there, I took off out the front door and explored. I met a maybe eight-year-old fellow called Barry Bates and with him a John Dozier, who looked the same age, and who I would discover soon enough was a street criminal at the soft age of eight. If there was an exploded frog in your mailbox, that was John Dozier's work. We were behind Barry Bates's house up on the back deck. Barry said to John, pointing to me, "He didn't go to school today." *"You didn't go to school today?"* John Dozier asked. Loudly. Next thing I knew, John's fingers were interlocked around my neck and he was choking me. At length. It was a perfect introduction to Plainview Drive. I'd been there eight hours and had been choked nearly to death by an eight-year-old with a future in a maximum-security institution. Welcome to the neighborhood.

* * * * * *

Sunday, May 27, 2012

DUI ran through my head all day the Sunday after it happened, that one word, or abbreviation, or whatever the fuck. I spent a lot of time on the phone apologizing to anyone who would listen—the band, Sack, random numbers out of the phone book, etc. I called a slew of friends just because I needed to spew the darkness out of my head. I talked with Marshall, Joe Elvis, Will. I had nice conversations with all of them. Then Darwin Colston, Esq., returned my call. He's the old fraternity brother and practicing lawyer. I was in for a shit sandwich, he said. His words. I took that to heart.

The family got invited over to Joe's to party like parents by the pool while the kids frolicked. I went along with the program but about 90 minutes into it I couldn't take it anymore. There wasn't enough distraction there to keep my mind from drifting off into thoughts of anal rape and getting fired, not to mention how much money this was all going to cost me. So Beth ran me home. "You were acting like you were passing a kidney stone for the whole time we were there," she said.

I watched *Lockup* and it wasn't nearly as fun as it usually is. I did the math on the whole weekend, wrote a lot of checks to musicians and agents, addressed a lot of envelopes, stamped them and walked them out to the mailbox. That kept me occupied. Beth came home but Nathan stayed over at Joe Elvis's house, no doubt having a ball. Beth is on the bed next to me watching a whole season of *Glee* that she recorded. I hate *Glee* more than mouth ulcers, but it ain't jail. And I like having her near right now. Even if she is pretty pissed.

* * * * * *

Tuesday, May 29, 2012

Hippie Jack called me twice today during an NA meeting. I stood outside the church talking to him and sweating great big wet splotches onto the light cotton bowling shirt I was wearing. He was helping me out. First thing, at his behest I had a new lawyer now, a local guy, and not some "big-city lawyer" who might piss the judge off just by being there. My new barrister's name was Pat Smith; the judge's name was John Smith, and he was my lawyer's uncle. In the realm of small-town justice, this sounded like a good thing.

Alternate Root magazine was doing a video special on the East Nashville music scene. So later that afternoon I sat in the sun in front of the Family Wash and played guitar and sang songs, sweating my shirt through some more. It made me feel good for a while, because if nothing else, I'm part of a music scene to the extent that somebody wants to shoot video of me.

I talked to Pat Smith on the phone. He charges a $1,000 flat fee and his modus operandi is to get continuance after continuance until he's managed to persuade the arresting officer to testify in favor of pleading the indictment down from a DUI to reckless driving or reckless endangerment. Lovely. Two more days' worth of Xanax, then two weeks 'til refill. Sweet Jesus. Where's that sharp knife we have?

* * * * * *

How do you get a songwriter off your front porch? Pay him for the pizza. What do you call a musician without a girlfriend? Homeless. How do you recognize the bride at a Hoosier wedding? The sequins on her bowling shoes. Why did the A&R man get hit by a train? He just didn't hear it. What's the last thing a stripper does to her asshole before going to work? Drops him off at band rehearsal. How many guitarists does it take to change a light bulb? Ten, one to change the bulb and nine to scoff and say, "Hell, *I* could have done *that!*"

* * * * * *

It is Friday, November 20, 2009. I'm 47 as of today and I'm rocking out. We're at Tidball's in Bowling Green and "I Don't Have a Gun" is sounding most excellent. I'm pretty sure it's Brad Pemberton on the drums, and I think that's Adam Fluher on the guitar; that's my main man Dan Seymour on the bass, and Lisa Oliver Gray, my sister from another mother, is up front singing with me. I'm having a fucking ball. My trusty battered Telecaster is nice to my fingers tonight and I'm nice back. The groove is good. It's a rock 'n' roll good time.

The guys have no clue that I've been flying on tabs all day and never more so than at this time onstage we have together. Lisa knows something, though. She is one of the best harmony singers alive. She pays attention. She watches every move my mouth makes and matches it; if I sing the wrong lyric, she's right there with me, and when it comes to onstage banter, the two of us can riff like Burns and Allen. She also knows me like a book. We've been singing together 20 years. And right now, she's on to me. All it takes for Lisa is one look at my pupils and she knows it's going to be one of "those" nights, nights when I don't make enough effort to connect with her, and seem to get lost in lyrics more often than not. But fuck it. This is rock 'n' roll, AND my birthday!

The gig is over and we are packing up our gear. I pack and stack my guitars and my amp and pedal board and harmonicas and merch case and then root around in my pockets for my car keys. They aren't there. They aren't on the stage. They aren't on any nearby table, and we now have a major threat to cognition.

I walk all the way out of the club the way I came in, my head down, scouring the floor looking for my keys. I walk out the front door into the cold November night, my eyes still trained on the ground, and I retrace my steps all the way to my car, where I discover it chugging merrily, thin wisps of exhaust dissipating quickly in the cold air. I have just played a 90-minute gig with my car running in the parking lot.

* * * * * *

November 25, 1968. Three days into my new life on Plainview Drive, Terry Cates reached into my shirt and twisted my nipple around so hard I thought it was going to come off. I was going to need to adjust and adapt.

It was a far cry from such great memories of Paducah, when I was four and scared to sleep alone, back when Mom would let me go to bed at 8 p.m. in her and Dad's bed, with the door open and the hall light on.

I could hear Dean Martin on the TV and that's when I had to go to bed, because Dean Martin was naughty. Lying in bed with the hall light on and hearing "Everybody loves somebody sometime," nestled under the covers and completely content and feeling safe.

That's the most secure I'd ever felt, until 16 years later when I first got stoned, as a junior in college, and, once the paranoia dissipated, felt that exact Dean Martin feeling. It was so wonderful. And that's what commenced my love affair with cannabis. Instant four-year-old feeling. The greatest feeling in the world.

* * * * * *

Saturday, July 21, 2012

I've been to Michigan, West Virginia, Florida, Kentucky, Ohio, Alabama, Florida, Texas, Mexico and Colorado in the last three weeks. Tonight in Fort Collins, Colorado, will be a house concert with Will Kimbrough and Brigitte DeMeyer, and tomorrow I get to fly home. I haven't been at work in three weeks and haven't coded a single goddam patient complaint; I don't even really know if I still have a job when I get back.

Last night Will and I played a duo show at the Sheridan Opera House in Telluride, Colorado. It was a ton of fun, great to play with him again. And now, he, Brigitte and I are on the way to Fort Collins. Only seven and a half hours of driving to go. I'm not on the rental insurance to drive, and just as well. Let them do it. I'll sit in the back and think the same thoughts over and over again.

Weeks before, I called Cumberland Heights, the drinking-and-drugging rehab center. But there was a problem with their taking Beth's Blue Cross, and I left it at that. At least I'd gone so far as to call them. It's a start, I told myself.

My travels before Colorado had been in Mexico. San Miguel de Allende, where Neal Cassady died running down the railroad trying to count the ties. There are a lot of American expats living the good life there, and Marshall Chapman has a fan base among them. She went down there maybe once a year to play house parties, and this time she wanted to bring me with her. It was a profoundly enlightening trip. It's utterly different from the United States. The poverty was palpable, and there is no middle class.

The first party, I killed it. Stone-cold sober, I played and sang great and ably backed Marshall up on what songs of hers I know. She was very happy. The next night we played another house where they had hash brownies. I ate a whole one before our show. Marshall told me later that I wasn't as on the ball as I was the night before, but I *was* funny as hell.

The next afternoon, I discovered you could get Xanax at a nearby apothecary, and that a doctor's office was down the street where you could get a prescription for Xanax basically by walking in and saying, "I'm nervous." In less than 30 minutes, I had scored 30 Xanax in a foreign country. That was cool as shit.

I was a very mellow guy when I showed up for our third and final gig of the trip, in a restaurant and bar this time. I was mellow unto the point of decomposition. Like usual I was convinced no one could see me belly up to the bar for a shot of tequila. I don't remember how many shots I had before the gig but I was invisible every time I dashed to the bar and downed one in a hurry. Marshall didn't see. Sure she didn't! I was on a lot of Xanax and was drinking alcohol on top of it. They warn you on the pill bottle not to do that. Worst-case scenario, you die; best case, you don't pass out in the middle of a song.

We got seated onstage. Before the first song, Marshall leaned over to me and said, "Are you alright?" I don't remember what I said back to her, but I probably drooled a bit when I said it. She started her first song and I joyfully joined in with a rhythm favored by drunks who take Xanax. She grimaced. That's all I remember of the show.

My plane the next morning was an early flight, so I had to wake up too early for comfort, and I was hovering in a twilight world: grievously hung over and still with a buzz on. I checked the Xanax bottle. It was empty. I had taken 30 Xanax in less than 24 hours, taken it with alcohol, too. I should be dead, but here I was, sitting somewhat upright, getting a ride to the airport.

My first flight was to Dallas. We were in the air. It was 10 a.m. and time to start drinking again. I'd like a Jack Daniel's, please, ma'am. Thank you so much. I drank my ass off on that plane. I've never been a very demonstrative drunk. I've never gotten aggressive or loud. I was always more the putting my arm around you and moaning "I love you, man!" type, so every time a flight attendant brought me another cute little bottle of Jack Daniel's, my thanks got more effusive. Thank you so very much! Oh, bless your heart, thank you, ma'am, so much!

I got off the plane in Dallas drunk out of my mind, with my backpack and my guitar. I'm surprised I could focus on the schedule screen well enough to find the gate to my flight to Colorado. I walked and walked and found my gate, and also a bar really near it! I bellied up to that bar instantly and resumed my binge. I continued it on the second flight. Thank you so very much, madam. You are SO SWEET! I don't even remember getting off the plane and getting my suitcase, but I do remember hooking up with Will and Bridgette. All I remember later is being in my bedroom in the condo the festival was putting us up in, and then getting a phone call. It was Cumberland Heights, and my insurance had been approved. I could start rehab as soon as was possible.

That was Friday, July 18, 2012. I haven't had a drink since.

what's the matter with him?!!

My learning to thrust and parry in Madisonville's children's demographic was a constant challenge. If kids were giving me a hard time just to see how I'd measure up, I'd interpret that as, "You don't like me and you don't want me around," and wind up not playing their game, and thus not be part of the crowd. As discussed earlier, I found humor. Somebody who's fucking with me cannot be dominant once I've made that person laugh. And the other kids giving me a hard time just became a normal inconvenience over time. Like everyone else, they were there to try out my comedy material on. That's what people became to me from then on through childhood, an audience to try jokes out on, not people. At the same time, I had a big personality and got great grades. Everybody wanted to copy my homework. I even got voted president of my fifth-grade class. I got laughter and applause in the seventh-grade school play, which totally changed my life. Then puberty hit and life went to shit.

All seventh-graders changed schools as we went on to Madisonville Junior High School for eighth and ninth grades. It seemed to me that the vibe of all the students changed. Everyone was irritable. A certain conviviality was gone. And there seemed to be new packs of beautiful people now, who only mixed with their own kind, and were irritated if someone beneath their station spoke to them. All the guys were irritable because they were dealing with their erections for the first time. Some were fast learners, and everybody was coming to grips with what horny felt like. I didn't even fully understand coitus until I read the Sonny Corleone and Lucy Mancini quickie passage in *The Godfather*. Lines like "blood engorged muscle" and "weeping, she gratefully took it into her wet turgid flesh" invited as many questions as answers. But that's how I learned about the birds and the bees: Mario Puzo.

In junior high, I was special even then. There was actually a function at school designed just to get a bunch of guys irritated at me all at the same time. Gym class. Forty young guys in maroon gym shorts and white T-shirts with MJHS printed on them, splitting up for teams to play volleyball. I could not hit any sort of ball and make it go anywhere you might want it to go, and I'd let the ball hit the floor as often as not. Thus would bring the cold, bracing invective down on my head. "You suck, man!" "You ain't no good." And here's how dumb I was, I kept trying new comedy bits on my teammates even as I was fucking up our chances of volleyball victory and all its glory. My bits fell flat. For my trouble, I got back, "Just shut up, Womack." "You're dumb, man!" "Damn faggot!" That class hurt. Over the next two years, I left a lot of self-esteem on that gleaming waxed basketball floor, but I didn't forsake honing my comedy chops, in this milieu concentrating on self-deprecation.

✶ ✶ ✶ ✶ ✶ ✶

It's March of 1979 and I'm 16 years old. It's a cloudy Saturday afternoon. I'm starring in the school play tonight. I just finished my $20-a-week job cleaning the church and I'm walking in the front door to get my play costume suit and then be right back out the door on my way to the school, to do the play, in the cafeteria, without a stage, because the intellectual bar at Madisonville North Hopkins High School is set so low, they didn't even build an auditorium. What's the point, right? AC/CD!!!

I'm accosted the moment I come in the front door. "Where have you been?" Mom exclaims. Dad actually levitates out of his recliner. "Son," he says approaching me, "You just about two hours LATE!"

"But, I was . . ."

Dad points a finger at me and says, "Shut it up."

"I was cleaning the church." I say. "Shut it up," he says.

"Well," Mom says, "you've had a friend who needs a ride to school with you tonight and he's been calling and calling."

"Uh, okay," I say, "it's probably Mike Regenold, I'll call him back."

Mom seems mollified or at least back to only normally hysterical. Dad, on the way back to his recliner, is not mollified. He's pissed off. "Boy, you made us worry!" he thunders as he sinks back into his seat.

Well . . . ," I stammer, "I'm sorry!"

I pass by Mom and go down the hall to my room, pick up my suit on a hanger, go to the phone in the kitchen, call Mike Regenold and come back through the living room on the way to the door. Mom is still standing near the door. "We just didn't know where you were," she says, placating. "Don't spoil on him," Dad grouses. "Boy's been spoiled on enough!" He then fixes me with a wicked stare and says, "Boy, I swear if you ever think about anybody besides yourself."

That hangs in the air a second. I run through my sins. I go to clean the church without telling anyone in an age before cellphones, I'm home in time to get my stuff, pick up Mike on the way, and be at the school on time. I didn't kill a baby, haven't started a fire. I just didn't let them know where I would be for one window of time in my day. But let's be frank. This is not just about today, is it? This is about cupcakes, brooding silence, walking on eggshells, not seeing the sense in praying just because it's dinnertime, the incessant television, which is on even as all this drama plays out.

I lay the suit down on a chair and face Mom, and in a halting, faltering voice dribbling with John Boy, I point to Dad and I say, "I hate to be disrespectful, but WHAT'S THE MATTER WITH HIM?"

The room freezes. Even the television sports announcer pauses.

"Everything's wrong!" I yell, choking back the tears that were coming. I have hardly asserted myself to anybody ever, and now here I am doing it, and I'm crying.

"Nothing's ever good!" I holler between sobs and wiping away tears and snot. "The house is sad! It's so sad! Every day it's like this. EVERY DAY! It never stops. Why can't this house just . . . be happy!" I sit down in the chair next to the door and I sob into my hands, my elbows on my knees. I cry long and hard, big rivers of tears and snot rolling down my face.

Mom is on my side now. Prayers have been answered. She's just glad that somebody finally said something about how we live—and she runs to fetch me some Kleenex and a glass of tap water. I sob for several moments, wiping my face, in that chair by the door. Dad just sits there. I'm out of the way of the television and he has apparently zoned back down the cathode rabbit hole. I wipe my eyes, blow my nose, pick up my suit, jingle the car keys in my pocket, and I'm out of there.

I pick up Mike and give no evidence I was so recently crying. Mike is a great guy who likes to laugh, so my material goes over well. We go to school, the play starts, we get through Act I fine, and then I go out of the cafeteria to the boys' bathroom down the hall to change into my suit and tie because Act II is when I wear it. I'm standing in front of a bathroom mirror putting on my necktie when Dad walks in. He and Mom have come to the play. And Dad's all dressed up.

There's a silence between us for a moment.

"You gettin' that necktie right?" Dad asks.

"I think so," I reply, coldly.

"Boy," he says, "you're the only one of the three boys ever learned how to tie a necktie." Then after a second, he leaves. I give it a moment, and then I leave too, going back out for Act II, to feel that intimacy you only get from strangers.

* * * * * *

Monday, August 6, 2012

I had to be there at Cumberland Heights Outpatient Recovery Center in Brentwood at 8 a.m. I'm allergic to 8 a.m., but like so much of rehab, it's not negotiable. I will come in the mornings, and code patient complaints at work in the afternoons.

The rest of the group would be there at 9, and I can just come in at 9 tomorrow, but today I had to have my pre-registration and interview and spill all my druggy secrets to Marita, the nice lady who greeted me when I came in. One great thing about rehab, or any recovery meeting—caffeine is never far away. "Would you like a cup of coffee?" Damn straight I would. Marita and I had a nice hour filling in forms and getting acquainted.

Group went well. I was the new kid in class and had an easy ride of it today. But I was noticeably depressed. Everybody went around the room telling their stories of where they are in their recovery, what they've been doing the last few days, what they haven't been doing that they should be doing, etc. I found that as sweet as Marita was in our first visit beforehand, she didn't take any shit. A couple of guys in the group were slacking and she called them out on it. Note to self: don't slack on Marita.

My homework? Walk around the block when I get home. I'm serious, walk around the block. (I'm pretty sure the assignments will get harder.) Marita had decided I needed some endorphins. So in the afternoon, I went to work and coded patient complaints for four or five hours and it couldn't have been more boring if it had been the Prince's Trust benefit concert with Eric Clapton, Phil Collins and Mark Knopfler. Then, when I got home, Nathan, the dog and I took that walk.

* * * * * *

My tearful takedown of Dad and his way of rapprochement compliment-ing my necktie ability didn't lead us into some new blossoming Ward and the Beaver relationship. But it did define us to each other a bit. You don't like me? Well, I don't like you, either. What do you think of that? I could watch my own black-and-white television in my room, and I could run my $65 white Kalamazoo SG electric guitar into a mic/line input on the back of my stereo, so I could play along with records as my guitar came through the speakers, too. Or I was typing the great American novel. I was a teenager, and teenagers spend a lot of time in their rooms, but there was a subtext to it in our house. Dad, you got your space, I got mine.

* * * * * *

"Why don't you just try it?"

I'm saying that with my fists balled up and staring down Pubic Enema Number One. I'm sixteen years old.

It's July 17th, 1979, and he's staring me down too, in his church pants and suspenders, slightly stooped like he's been ever since the triple bypass of '77. He's come down the hallway to my bedroom because I've been throwing a big-ass fit. That's been my thing lately, throwing fits. I'm angry a lot of the time. I think what got his attention from down the hall in the living room was the noise I made throwing a chair across my room and both breaking the chair and putting a hole in my closet door.

"Son, push me any farther and I swear I'll take you down a peg even if it puts me in my grave!"

"Why don't you just try it?"

"Shut it up, boy! Just shut it up!"

We stare each other down for another second. And then it's over. He turns around and leaves my room. I let him go with having the last word. I haven't been in a fight since the rinky-dink scuffles I and the other little neighborhood kids had when we were very young. Anyway, I can see how it would look in the Madisonville Messenger. *"Healthy 16 Year-Old Kicks Heart Patient's Ass." That wouldn't play in Peoria.*

* * * * * *

I was 16. At night I'd drive around in circles at the shopping center, cruising with all the other kids, occasionally pulling over into parking spaces for conversations and finding out if anybody knew anybody who could get some beer. Eric Ramsey or Mike Howard would show up and I'd park my own car and ride around with them. Other nights I drove alone all over town without cruising the shopping center once. There was a bridge next to a church on the north side of town and sometimes I'd be crying and trying to work up the nerve to drive off the side of that bridge. I'd crisscross that bridge six times sometimes, smearing tears and snot on the steering wheel.

It wasn't always just over some girl, either. It was me sometimes thinking, maybe my material's just not improving, maybe I'll never ever really become a funny guy, or even a liked guy, or an accepted guy. The world needs ditch diggers too. This is life? What's the point? Especially when your heart's been broken repeatedly with a claw hammer. You don't even know when it's coming, but you'll get that empty "what's the point?" for a few minutes. You tell jokes or listen to records, you tape-record Monty Python episodes and transcribe the Doug and Dinsdale Piranha sketch and learn it by heart. You tape Casey Kasem's "American Top 40" and for a flashback they play "Louie Louie" and you learn to play it by practicing with that cassette for hours—to get through those times. That's what you do.

* * * * * *

Saturday, August 11, 2012

I played the Tomato Fest in East Nashville this afternoon with my band, complete with horn section. No Xanax. It was one of those gigs where I'm hating everything that comes out of my mouth and guitar and for some reason everybody out in the audience appears to be liking it. Everybody told me it was great. A guitar hero of mine was there, and apropos of nothing he said I could call him any time if I needed to. He was a friend of Bill W. Somehow he knew.

I was the cocktail weenie before the main course: Elmo Buzz and the East Side Bulldogs, which was Todd Snider, Elizabeth Cook, Tim Carroll, Paul Griffith, Eric McConnell, and special guest Bobby Keys on saxophone. Bobby Keys of the Rolling Damn Stones. There he was behind the stage before the show, standing in the dark away from everybody else, smoking a joint alone. A legend alone. There I was 10 feet away, drinking Diet Coke out of a plastic bottle. Even if he hadn't been smoking weed I don't know if I'd have approached him. I get a kick out of seeing heroes around town and a bigger kick out of meeting them, but when I see them like I see Bobby Keys tonight, or pass Buddy Miller on the street, *or have Emmylou Harris seated next to me for an entire Ray Davies concert*, I feel like the best gift I can give them is just to leave 'em be.

I planed off the Xanax this week, and haven't had one since Wednesday. I'd give my left nut for one. If you tapped me on the shoulder right now I'd hop a foot in the air. My stomach is upset but—all told—I'm not really unhappy. I played a good gig with my band and a guitar hero friend of mine told me to call him anytime, although the last thing I would ever dream of doing is to actually call him and ruin it. I'd just done my first gig sober.

* * * * * *

My days for all of August into mid-September were 9 to noon at Cumberland Heights learning things about myself, and then 1 or so to 5 or so I would go to Vanderbilt and . . . endure, slapping myself in the face to keep up and pay attention to each new patient's bitching about how the doctor had kept him waiting, or misdiagnosed her or accidentally amputated his nose or *who the fuck cares?*

Then I'd go home and do my rehab homework. There was always homework. One daily one was a checklist of how you've felt today plus any comments about good or bad things for that day. We did that one every night. On top of that I have a bigger assignment due, which basically involves writing down every resentment I've ever had and, somehow in conjunction with that, every last fucked-up, stupid or just plain mean stunt I've ever pulled. Every damn last instance. Beth would be asleep next to me and I'd be scribbling down disgusting things about myself late into the night.

I grew to really like the rehab meetings. I guess because I was really ready this time. Drugs and booze had kicked my ass and I was a good student. It was in a nicely done room that could fit 15 people seated on the perimeter so we could all see each other. The summer sun would come in through windows set high on the outside wall. And the air conditioning was just right. Unlike Parthenon Pavilion, it was a room designed with a fucked-up person's actual sensitivities in mind. Marita sat up front and ran things. We'd go around the room giving our daily report, how we felt, what's been up, etc.

It was an interesting group: a jovial retired broker named Brian who'd been drinking for 50 years and was desperate to stop; a housewife named Carla whose marriage was on the rocks because she just couldn't stay out of the wine bottle until she passed out; Rachel, who came in dressed very corporate every day because she immediately left afterward to go to her straight job, which she couldn't afford to lose because she was trying to regain custody of her young son. Drugs had brought Rachel down. Meth and pain pills.

Heroin was Jade's problem. (None of these are real names.) She was a seriously hot dancer who danced on bar tops for tips in a club uptown and made good money. Her man would meet her there when she needed to cop. Wendell was a charming musician who actually worked steady, but when he wasn't gigging he had the odd compulsion to just sit in his bedroom with the door shut doing cocaine all day long. He was married with a young son, who was on the other side of Wendell's bedroom door, somewhere, having a life without his daddy. Layla was a sweetheart. She was a married mother of three who had smoked marijuana all day every day for 20 years. I got a hug from her on our first meeting. With no thought of it, she would stand and go write something positive or life-affirming, or just plain opaque, on the blackboard.

There were many others who came and went. The guy in the cap who didn't say much. The guy in a suit who was trying to stay employed and save his boozehound skin at the same time. The really young rich kid who deep down didn't seem to comprehend that he had a problem. Some of them were graduating when I got there, or were new when I was graduating. It was never-ending; the room changed almost every day by at least one person, but the people who started around the same time I did, Wendell, Brian, Rachel, Carla, we grew close over the next few weeks.

* * * * * *

In high school, by senior year, fall of 1979, I went to Mom with things like this: "Mom, I don't want to live anymore." I can't imagine how hearing that made her feel. There's no pain like your child's pain, I remember her telling me that once.

She found me a counselor to go see out at Trover Clinic. She kept it off Dad's radar, paying cash for the visits. I found out Mom was paying $50 in cash each time I saw this lady. This is the Mom who fed a family on $30 a week. She reused strips of aluminum foil, *she had a box labeled "bits of string too small to use"!* She didn't have the resources to keep this is up. So I did what I had to do. I faked getting better. The visits WERE helping, and I was feeling better for real, but I amped it up for public consumption. "Mom, I don't need to see this lady anymore. I feel like I want to live now." I continued my rambling cruising all over town and thinking about that railroad bridge, isolated myself in my bedroom playing the guitar and typing, and don't you know at school I could be the funniest, knee-slappingest cut-up you ever met, smiling big like an idiot. Picking my nose like I'd left a goddam nickel up there.

little miracles

I bought my first guitar, a Stella acoustic, from Vicky Smith up the street in June 1978. I paid her $18 for it. It came with a Mel Bay chord book and a songbook but of course her little brother Layne Alan also provided me with the Kiss "Rock & Roll Over" chord songbook. The first chords I ever learned to play were the intro to "Calling Dr. Love"—E, G, D, A, in that order. Good chords to know.

I made a strap out of twine and proceeded to live with that Stella, either on my person or within reach, for years. I began with no clue what I was doing, and there was no one to show me. So I researched. If there was a guitar player on television, I watched him or her. I picked up this chord or that one, but it was a slow process. And it hadn't escaped me that the sounds I was hearing on Kiss and Cheap Trick records were not sounds I could get out of an 18-fret Stella acoustic guitar.

To that end, the following summer, I paid $63 for an electric white Kalamazoo SG model. I had made the happy discovery that there was a "mic" input on the back of my stereo that would accommodate a quarter-inch guitar cable. I learned a few things off records here and there, but again, I was flying solo. My prowess might have improved at a better clip if I had known someone else who played, or if I didn't split my time between the guitar and the typewriter. But one day somebody showed me how to make barre chords, and that was a revelation.

I could not sing at all. So I never really *learned* songs all the way through. I just learned licks off them. There was no reason ever to learn how to play a song all the way through. I wasn't in a band, I wasn't jamming with friends, or otherwise playing publicly, but I was learning licks and I was having a ball trying to learn Cheap Trick songs and Clash songs. The first guitar lead I ever learned was the one on "Police and Thieves," during the snowy January of 1980.

Then I went off to Western Kentucky University and found people to play with, and the learning curve went up. One main reason I pledged a fraternity was Bill Brown, he of God-talking-through-a-supply-closet-door fame, who could play the fire out of a guitar and put bands together for parties. I learned a lot from him. I learned "Twist and Shout," "I Saw Her Standing There," "Honky Tonk Women," "Take It Easy." I fancied myself more of a punkier rebel who wanted to do Clash songs, but I couldn't pull it off, not musically or visually, preppy myopic dweeb that I was, so I was happy to learn songs and play in a band and drink beer at a party. It was a lot of fun.

It was around this time in my life that Waymond came home to visit and Dad mused to him in laconic Arkansas style: "If that boy ain't careful he's gonna learn how to play that guitar."

* * * * * *

And then there was 1981. And Lori. My first-ever real girlfriend. Even the losers get lucky sometimes.

She was younger than me. I was 18 in college, she was 16 in high school. The summer of '81 we dated and I guess we did a few things both for the first time together. I really liked her, and it was mutual. Then I went off for my sophomore year of college and didn't really so much dump her as callously freeze her out. I was entranced with the female talent on tap in college and hadn't much in the way of empathy and character in those days. I tried a couple of times later in the semester to maybe get back with Lori on the odd weekend trip home. And then, by the next summer break in '82, I'd wormed my way back into her heart and we were a couple again, for the rest of summer. I had a new feeling with her; I didn't feel like she was above my station or unattainable. It just felt nice.

But I can remember the moment I fell head-over-heels in love with her. We were lying on a blanket under a big sycamore tree at the Madisonville City Park in August 1982, and she told me her high school GPA was 3.9 going into what would be her senior year. I know how bizarre this is, but when she mentioned that she had paper proof of how smart she was, that turned me on! A high school GPA turned me on. Honest to God.

Within days of that moment, I had idealized her, and I fell head-over-heels in love with my newly idealized vision of Loriness. I'm fairly certain my behavior toward her changed. And by the time fall semester came around, the bloom was off the rose a bit—for her! I could kind of tell. This was a problem, inasmuch as now without her I couldn't breathe, without her life meant nothing. Without her how can I put up with the fact that I'll never be in a cool rock band?

I went back off to college in late August '82, utterly smitten. I wrote her every week, I sent her cards, I played a lot of guitar, drank a lot of beer and studied my ass off. I had a pathetic notion that maybe if my GPA were better, it would make me more worthy of Loriness. (I wound up getting a 3.6 that fall semester.) I made it back home as many weekends as I could to see her, but more and more she had things she needed to do that weekend that didn't include me. I could see the writing on the wall and in my diseased brain I felt the best thing for me to do would be to accost Lori in my car in the cinema parking lot after we'd just seen *Tootsie* and tell her (and I quote), "I love you so much I could just shit!"

Her response was measured, diplomatic and included, "I do love you but I am just feeling the need to . . . not commit too heavily into a relationship." I was devastated. Immediately. It didn't take any time at all.

I stayed devastated too, and not just over Lori, Staci, Tina, alienation, blinking, being the class freak then a frat boy, and dreaming of being in a band and dreaming of being a writer. I was clinically depressed. At the age of 20, I was tired. I was tired of being desperate for attention and my neck HURT goddammit. All the head jerking and blinking all these years. I was tired of being a square peg even at the age when square pegs are beginning to find where they fit. I was tired of desperately needing to be funny, or smart, or cool. I'd had it.

I know, I know, *boo-fucking-hoo. She doesn't like you anymore! Your daddy didn't want your cupcake! Poor, poor Tommy!* Yeah, yeah, fuck off. It was the only life I knew, with nothing to compare it to, and I wanted out.

* * * * * *

Thursday, August 23, 2012

I read my 20 Consequences in group today. That's where you list out the top 20 shittiest, stupidest, meanest, most destructive things you've ever done in your entire substance-riddled life. It's not pretty, or fun. I'd already watched some of the others read theirs, and it's hard to reconcile the nice persons you know with the horrible things they recount, reading from their sheets of paper and breaking down crying.

You take a sheet of paper, or eight, list what you did, whom it affected, and how you feel about it. You take your time and you rack your brain to recall the crappiest things you've ever done. Then you take it to group and read it in front of everybody, and the only thing that makes it any easier is that you're reading it to relative strangers, and their own stories remind you that you're far from being the first person who's fucked up in horrible ways.

I had three sheets of paper, written on front and back in my florid, first-draft style, with lots of extra adjectives and run-on sentences. I know that you, the reader, already know I've done some stupid shit, but you only know what I've told you about. There's other shit.

I read aloud stuff I'd never mentioned to anyone, until that day, in that room at Cumberland Heights, with a dozen other recovering alcoholics and addicts listening to me. I don't know if I'm supposed to feel better, or even good, after such a recitation. But I do feel that a few things that have been rattling around in my soul have been brought out into the sun. What were plums can now melt into prunes.

* * * * * *

It is December 2009, I think. Molly Thomas and I are backing up Todd Snider at the Mercy Lounge and we get to open up the show as well. She does a set and then I do a set and then we all play backing up Todd. I'm playing my Telecaster. It's a delicate thing to do, an electric guitar in an ensemble with an acoustic guitar and a fiddle, with no drums and bass to hide your mistakes. You've got to be right on the beat, your tone has to be tight and cutting through the mix, and you've got to play like everyone in the building can hear every mistake you make, because they can.

It's one of those gigs where I just don't fuck up much. I'm not drinking or smoking but I do have a Xanax and one pain pill in my pocket. I'm timing when I take them so I can hit the stage at maximum ecstasy. Elvis, Todd's road manager, asks if I could cut my set down to 25 minutes from 40. I'm pissed but I assent to it, and later on I'll be very grateful to him because it turns out that 25 minutes is exactly the right amount of time for me to go out and absolutely obliterate a packed house of Todd Snider fans, some of whom are my fans, too. They want to like me and I want to be liked. And I only need 25 minutes to do it right and not overstay my welcome.

I'm solo but I'm playing electric guitar. Like Billy Bragg. It makes everything rock a little more but you have to be careful with the strummy songs. What I'll mainly remember from this night is "Alpha Male & the Canine Mystery Blood," and how quiet 400 people can get. I play the same palm-muted chords over and over again, with no changes, E, B, D, A, while I speak-sing my life story. It's wide-ranging, it's funny, it tugs at the heart, and it's eight minutes long. Eight minutes of holding 400 people in the palm of my hand, the torrent of words never letting up except for pauses after the lines that get the laughs. I'm killing them. KILLING them! And then it's over. All too soon, which is perfect. They want more and they're not going to get it. I take very long bows at the last considerable ovation. And I'm thinking, Nights like this. They come along just often enough.

* * * * * *

It was around December 20, 1982. I was home from college. I was a puddle of a human who got a 3.6 GPA that semester because I thought a GPA was sexy. I called Loriness to see if I could come by and bring her a Christmas present. "Oh . . . well, can we get together tomorrow night?" She hadn't gotten me anything yet.

I hadn't brought my stereo home with me from the frat house where I was vice president of the place now. (A fraternity vice president who wants to be in a rock band. That's rich.) But Sissie's old Panasonic stereo was still set up in what was still her bedroom when she was home for holidays. I would put records on that stereo and just stand there. I wouldn't sit down on the bed. I would just stand on the carpet next to the stereo. And if I wanted to hear a song on a 12-inch album again because it sounded so good, I would pick up the needle and with great windstorm noises move it back to the song's beginning.

I had Elvis Presley's first RCA album, Marshall Crenshaw's *Field Day*, Stevie Ray Vaughn's first album, *London Calling, The Kinks are the Village Green Preservation Society*, Bruce Springsteen's *The River* and a few others. I would walk in the front door past Mom and Dad watching television, go straight back to Sissie's bedroom and listen to records, standing by the stereo, hands in pockets, looking down at the carpet. I would be in there for hours without changing my position. I did this the night of the 21st too, and again on the 22nd, when I got back home after I'd awkwardly exchanged gifts with Loriness and shared a kiss or two without much feeling to them. I came home and went back to the stereo, standing there listening endlessly to Elvis's "I'm Gonna Sit Right Down and Cry Over You," not because of the lyrical content, but because it was a great rock 'n' roll performance by masters: Elvis,

Chet Atkins, Scotty Moore, D.J. Fontana, Bill Black and Floyd Cramer. It's a profoundly great track.

And that's what I was listening to when the bedroom door opened and in came Mom and Dad. It's not like they hadn't noticed, and they had seen it a lot over the years, but this time was different. This time I was scary.

I turned down the stereo as if I knew we were going to have a serious conversation.

Dad spoke after a minute, and I honestly don't know what he said, but I can remember a kindness in his voice I had never heard before. A silence fell, as I took in a deep breath. I was about to say something that would devastate them both.

"Mom, Dad," I said, "I hate to tell you this, and I know it's the last thing you'd ever want to hear. But I honestly don't want to live any longer. If this is it, if this is life, I don't think I want anything more to do with it."

My words were like a lead weight levitating in the air. There was nothing they could say for a few moments. Mom had the most worried look on her face. Then Dad came up to me a step. He reached up his right hand, and put it on my right shoulder. He touched me. With his hand. He looked at me. It was a different face.

"Son, would you go see a psychiatrist if we can find one?"

". . . Sure," I mumbled, I think.

I went back to listening to "I'm Gonna Sit Right Down and Cry Over You" as if they weren't there. And in a few moments they left the room. About five minutes later, Dad came back in. He put his hand on my shoulder again, and he said, "Son, Maw and I just want you to know that we love you, and we'll help you however we have to."

He left me to my Elvis, which I took off the turntable and replaced with Marshall Crenshaw because "Whenever You're on My Mind" is a glorious kill-all to any bad feelings you might have, for as long as it lasts. But it hadn't escaped me that Dad had touched me with his hand and told me he loved me. In other words, who are you and what have you done with Dad?

Two nights later, Christmas Eve, about 10:30, I sat in the dark in my own bedroom, on the edge of the bed, the only light coming from the plastic Christmas candles shining through the window, and I had a bottle of prescription antihistamines in my hand. Mom's. I was now about to become the first person to try overdosing on allergy medication.

With a glass of sweet iced tea on my dresser top, I took some of the pills and chased them with the official Southern beverage, and then

I took some more and washed them down. I sat there in the darkness some more, and took one last gulp of three or four pills. Then I thought about frying in a lake of fire for eternity like a slice of country ham.

I drove myself to the emergency room at the Regional Medical Center, told them what I'd done, and they gave me some ipecac, which reverses gear in the stomach to get up and gone whatever down there needs to come out. There was a clock on the wall. 11:55 p.m. I watched the clock turn from Christmas Eve to Christmas as I threw up in a tub in the downtown ER.

They wouldn't let me drive myself home. So Dad came and got me. "Dad," I said, "I'm more trouble than I'm worth."

"Don't worry about it, Son," he said, like an Arkansan hick Mike Brady, "and you're no trouble at all, Son. None at all."

* * * * * *

Tuesday August 28, 2012

Step Two: We came to believe a power greater than ourselves could restore us to sanity.

I am going through something extraordinary. I haven't had a Xanax since August 12, over two weeks ago. They are known to be hell to kick. It traditionally takes a month or more for the worst of it. I am certainly familiar with what it feels like to go that long without one of my little pink jewels. I know all about the tightness in your throat, the sour stomach, the sense of dread, and some dark spot inside you screaming bloody murder.

What I'm not familiar with is how I feel right now, two weeks after my last Xanax, which is . . . okay. I'm really okay. My chest isn't tight, I'm able to eat, and I've caught myself on numerous occasions actually not even thinking about it. I've had a lifetime of Bibles thumped on my head, prayed my knees off and crucified my G.I. Joe, but I don't know that I've ever experienced anything closer to God than right now. Something is making it okay not to have Xanax in my system, and the only thing I'm sure of is that something isn't me. I'm not doing this.

* * * * * *

The SG guitar back in the early days had a shitty upper neck. I could never really wail at the 12th fret. So during college I traded it for a Fender Musicmaster, one of their budget models. The 12th-fret action wasn't much better than the SG's, but I made the best of it. A year later I found a damaged but playable Gretsch Rally. This guitar sounded wonderful, but strings tended to get caught on the screws rising out of the pickups, and I had yet to get a guitar with a great neck that I could really improve on. Still, I was learning things. I was even copping Brian Setzer and Stevie Ray licks.

I had a Yamaha acoustic guitar now (a step up) and I was really catching on with it. I'd actually play whole songs for all the others on the front porch of the frat house; I was singing these songs too. In a low-volume, unconfident voice. It was easier to sing with another good voice, like Rufus Baker's, when we sang "Feelin' Groovy" together, or Bill Brown and me doing "Love Me Do." I could also play "Alice's Restaurant," complete with the correct picking pattern and all the words. I could do "Fire and Rain" with all the guitar playing pretty damn correct. "Alice's Restaurant" impressed people, that I can remember all those words. "Fire and Rain" will get you laid.

* * * * * *

Dad knew who he wanted to get me in to see. He wasn't a psychiatrist, he was a social worker, and on the weekends he preached at a Cumberland Presbyterian Church somewhere out in the boonies. His office was in Hopkinsville. This was Dr. Arthur Burroughs, the man I would see for the next two years and who would pronounce me an alcoholic at the end of our time together. He owed Dad a big favor, apparently, something about Dad's saving him from getting defrocked after a dispute with parishioners. I don't know for sure, but it was a serious enough favor Dr. Burroughs owed Dad that he saw me once a week for two years and never charged us a penny. I felt like I had at last found somebody to talk to. So we talked once over the Christmas holiday, then I went back to college in January, and every Saturday morning I'd drive on two-lane US 68-80 from Bowling Green to Hopkinsville, see Dr. Burroughs, unload on him, and be back in Bowling Green by 1 p.m.

It was a very difficult spring semester. I spent a lot of time alone with my guitars and sometimes breaking into crying spells. I was still profoundly in love with my dear idealized version of Lori, even as the relationship had petered out.

Bill Brown had graduated and so had his repertoire of the Beatles, Cars and Eagles. The band was now Scott Willis and Ken Flaherty on guitars, me on a rented bass and Greg Curry on drums. And the repertoire had changed to the Ramones, Johnny Thunders and Robert Gordon. We played some righteous parties in the Sig Ep basement and those were fun moments, jewels in a road paved with shit. The reason I played rented bass was that Scott and Ken had much better guitars than I had. I was the better player, but they could wheedly-whee on their 12th frets and I couldn't.

I would sometimes call home in crying fits from pay phones and just tie Mom and Dad's stomachs into knots. I had no desire to hurt them. These bawling calls were not made out of revenge for growing up in an unhappy home. They were bona fide cries for help. Dr. Burroughs couldn't prescribe medications, and no medical doctor was ever sought to look into whether there was something that might help me. I needed something. There should have been something, but it didn't really compute with anybody, including me.

✶ ✶ ✶ ✶ ✶ ✶

So the spring semester ended. I had a new job that summer of '83, courtesy of Dad. I was custodian of the Cumberland Presbyterian church camp, Camp Koinonia, in the tiny hamlet of Logansport, Kentucky, about 40 minutes north of Bowling Green. This was the camp where I had fallen in love with Brenda Collins all those years ago.

Dad was very active in the camp, always had been. And he and I spent a lot of time together getting the buildings ready. I had a little bed and bath in one basement corner of the big house, where the cafeteria was and where the canteen was, with the revival hall upstairs, which from the front was the first floor.

I set up shop in my bedroom. I had a guitar amp, a little eight-watt Fender Champ that got the job done, and my Gretsch Rally. Lame high action or not, there was still a lot I could do on that guitar, and I was playing the heck out of it. In the revival hall, I found a record turntable with a 16 rpm speed setting, and every electric guitarist back then knew that if you slowed a 33 1/3 rpm record down to 16, all the notes were an exact octave down and at the slower speed so you could more easily figure out flashy lead licks and complicated riffs. I stole that turntable and set it up in my room. My quest was to learn how to play "Double Talking Baby" by the Stray Cats, "Stray Cat Blues" by the Stones, "All Day and All of the Night" by the Kinks and a slew of other ones. If I wasn't doing custodial things for the campers—replacing light bulbs, unstopping toilets, etc.—I was playing guitar.

I remember running the riding mower over all the campgrounds, and when I was done, Dad was standing at my ending spot. He was in a short-sleeve business shirt and a tie, suspenders holding up his church pants, and he said, "Son, you mowed that grass real good."

Later I had to turn three large garbage containers on their sides and hose out the entire funk in the bottoms of them, the sour milk, stuck-on food and other smelly deposits. I got the hose, a bucket of soapy water, and a couple of rags and I went to work on them. When I was done, Dad said, "Son, those dumpsters haven't looked that good in years."

At night after vesper services, Dad was bringing preachers into my room and asking me to play guitar for them. "Play that 'I Wanna Play House With You' one," he'd say. So I would play Elvis's "Baby Let's Play House" and Dad would tell the preachers, "You give this boy a while and he can make that guitar talk to ya."

* * * * * *

Wednesday, August 29, 2012

Sack and I broke up today. I mean business-wise. We met for coffee and she lowered the boom. It has as much to do with the economy as anything; we're just not making much money. She's wondering how she's going to make her bills, thinking about becoming a temp. But my behavior is also a factor in her decision. She's had enough.

It was a good ride. Five years. I owe her a lot. I'm flush with good feeling from doing something positive, going to rehab, so I think that's easing the sting. I don't know what I'm going to do. But one thing they're always harping on in recovery circles is "just for today." Yesterday's gone—tomorrow might not happen. Just deal with today. Today's a pretty, sunny day. Hot! But if you don't like hot you might ought to leave Nashville. I'm not too seared by the knowledge that I dug my own grave with Sack. It'll probably bother me later. Things always take a while to sink in with me. It is what it is. Today I'm all right.

* * * * * *

It was August of '83. All the church camps ended three weeks before I had to be back to school. So I folded up shop and headed home to stay for the duration. I was bummed as hell all the time because it had become normal for me to be that way. It was no longer a bump in the road, it was who I was.

One day I wandered into one of my favorite places in the Best Town on Earth *(kiss my aisse!)*, Don's House of Music on Center Street. He stocked good guitars, name brands: Gibsons, Fenders, Martins, cool shit. Amps too.

There were two Telecasters on the wall. I admired them because they were the go-to axe of so many cool songwriters and band leaders I admired. It appeared to be the guitar that provided a foundation. And you can play leads on them, too. Jimmy Page proved it.

One of the Telecasters was sky blue. I didn't really like that color, so I picked up the other one, an off-white, cream-colored beauty, and sat down with it, plugging it into the nearest amp. A guitar lead I'd always loved was Keith Richards's intro on the Stones' "Time Is on My Side." It has great bends and bluesy cool phrasing and it swings, too. But the Keith intro starts at the 12th fret and goes all the way to the 15th fret. I KNEW what the notes were, I'd just never had an instrument on which I could play them. With that Telecaster I sat down and played the intro to "Time Is On My Side" exactly right, for the first time in my life. I nearly cried.

I got lost in that guitar for maybe 20 or 30 minutes, sounding better than I ever had in my life. I fell in the love with the neck, and how much easier it was to fret my chords. Oh, my. Then suddenly reality struck and my mood came crashing down. I was in love with this guitar; therefore I'd never have it, because it was too good for me. It was no use. I resolutely unplugged it, switched off the amp, hung the Telecaster back on its spot on the wall, walked out of the store and drove home dejected.

I walked in the front door and there was Dad in his recliner, watching some television. I sat down in a chair because maybe it was something we could watch together. It wasn't really, but it didn't matter because Dad muted it almost immediately. "How's it going, Son?" It wasn't so long ago it would have been "Hey, boy." Now, it's "How's it going, Son?"

"It's going," I replied.

"Where you been?" he asked.

"Well, I went down to Don's and I played this one guitar he's got in there and it was like a beautiful dream. I could play 'Time Is On My Side' on it!" (Like he'd even know what that song was!) "I swear, Dad, that guitar was beautiful, but so out of my league financially that I'll never have one. But it sure was so much easier to sound good when I played it." The room was silent for a moment. "Oh, well," I sighed.

"Well," Dad said after a moment, "there's some dinner left over for you in the fridge."

A couple of days went by, and one afternoon I was in my bedroom with the door closed listening to the stereo, reading a *Creem*. There was a knock on the door and in walked Dad. He sat down on the foot of my bed and faced me. It was still weird seeing him not completely without the frown, but with concern. I reached over and turned the stereo down. We made small talk, I don't remember, but it wasn't long before the topic became guitars. "So you feel like you'd be a better guitar player with that guitar down at Don's?" Dad asked me. "Oh, yeah," I said, "no question." "Well," he said, sitting there in his summertime uniform of short sleeves, necktie, and suspenders, "what if you had that guitar?"

* * * * * *

September 19, 2012

I coined out of Cumberland Heights yesterday morning. What that means is that everybody in my group passed around my gold-looking coin symbolizing my achievement, and while they had it in their hands, said a few words about me. There were a lot of kind words. My meds don't let me cry. But I was close to it. I'm going to miss those people; I'm going to miss that room.

I can't believe I'm 35 days clean. I haven't been 35 days clean—of everything!—for almost 30 years. I think I've always believed I couldn't or wouldn't ever get this far. For the first time, I'm doing it right: going to meetings, calling my sponsor, reading the Big Book, praying, meditating some, putting my sobriety above everything else. I'm on what they call the Pink Cloud, a feeling of elation common in early recovery. I don't know how long it will last, but I'm enjoying the hell out of it.

* * * * * *

The next afternoon after Dad and I talked about the guitar, Dad asked me to take a ride with him. He steered us to Don's House of Music. We walked in and Dad asked me which was the guitar I fancied. I pulled that beautiful off-white Fender Telecaster off its peg on the wall and showed it to him. "Well, come on, then." He said. The next thing I knew, Dad was at the front counter, had opened up his checkbook and was fishing out his fountain pen. And Don was putting this beautiful guitar in a case, and the list price for a Telecaster in 1983 was $450. Dad did not have $450 ever. I don't know how or what he had to do to get enough money into his checking account to walk up to Don and write one check to cover everything but that's what he did, and no more than 10 minutes after we'd walked into Don's, we walked out the front door on a beautiful, sunny summer day, and I owned that Fender Telecaster.

My Dad, that old cantankerous cuss, all emotionally detached, he went to bat for me. He made a big-money bet that I would actually play this thing and go somewhere with it. For a moment, we stood by the car, him on the left driver's side and me on the other side, the guitar case in the back seat, and we just looked at each other for a second. Then we went home, picking our noses.

* * * * * *

At some point around this time, Dad and I took off together around 7 a.m. and went to a river back near Kentucky Lake where we used to go for fun. He was taking me fishing. A 65-year-old father and a 20-year-old son, sitting in a boat casting toward the shore in order to seduce young bluegills and crappies. Dad caught way more than I did. I wasn't making much conversation and Dad of all people took up the slack.

"Yeah, Son," he said, "fishin', it ain't much, but I sure do enjoy it."

I enjoyed it, too. Not just enjoyed it, I was amazed. Dad, damaged as he was, was working as hard as he possibly could to be nice, and giving, and loving. To make up time, to make now matter. He never worked this hard in the Bethel College years. Sixty-five years old with a triple bypass behind him, a mountain in his mind nobody could climb, and the wonderful cuss took me fishing. They say old dogs can't learn new tricks. But Dad did.

epilogue:

the things you learn in the back of a room

It is Monday night, November 20, 2012. My 50th birthday. I am center stage, playing and singing my masterpieces to a surprisingly large audience at 3rd & Lindsley in Nashville. With me are my dear mates. Daniel Seymour is on bass, and Justin Amaral is on drums, Mark Robinson's roiling his swampy electric guitar, Michael Webb is on keys and Hammond organ and even Jim Hoke is here, the man who can play instruments that haven't even been invented yet, and he's brought his sax and a pedal steel tonight. (Ya gotta love a cat who has chops on pedal steel and saxophone both.)

On the harmony vocals and the occasional lead-vocal turn is my sister from another mother, one of the most spiritually clued-in people I've ever known. The intelligent, angel-voiced, perfect comic and harmony partner with me gig after gig, Lisa Oliver Gray.

Like on every electric gig I play, I'm playing the Telecaster. It's not off-white anymore; years of smoky bars have turned it yellow like my teeth. It's beat to shit. There are chips and paint missing in various parts of the body, but it plays great. It's got different pickups in it, it's had three different bridges and it's been refretted twice. But it's still basically the same beast, with the flattest, smoothest neck I've ever seen on a Tele. Never seen another Fender neck like it. I played it in Government Cheese, I played it in the bis-quits, I've played it in England and Sicily. Dad did the nicest thing anyone's ever done for me. And I play this guitar for him, for me and for as many people I can. I've played this guitar for coming up on three decades. For years I would randomly call home and tell Dad, "I just had to call and thank you for the guitar," and he would always say, "Son, you're as welcome as the flowers in May!" After April 2000, I couldn't call and thank him anymore. He died Easter weekend. Like a preacher.

I haven't had a drink or a drug in four months, I have a sponsor, I'm going to meetings, I'm working the program for really the first time ever, and the improvement in my whole life in four short months has been massive. Changes happen overnight sometimes. I go to bed as this one guy and I wake up with some new insight on how to handle some sort of bullshit. All day long I feel knots unraveling.

A door has opened. For years now I hadn't ever been listening to music anymore. I'd drive from gig to gig alone in the car with no music playing at all, because my guilty conscience insisted that my attention be focused on everything bad I'd ever done. Tommy. You're an asshole and here's another reason why! When you run a rickety electric fan for hours in a house, it's noisy but becomes just a part of your life; you don't even hear it after a while, until somebody finally turns the fan off and the resultant instant peace and quiet shows how unsettling the fan had been all that time. Well, right around this birthday night, the fan turns off. Silence. Hawkeye, Hot Lips, the shelling stopped. I'll start to have room in my brain to enjoy music again. And I'll enjoy it like it's a reunion with some wonderful old friend. I'll get up in the attic and retrieve the old-school jam box and I'll sit it on the floor next to my shower. I'll soap and rinse to tunes. I'll cue up the iPad and fire up the Bluetooth speaker, blasting the Sonics while I load the dishwasher.

In February 2013 the whole DUI thing will resolve in bumfuck municipal court. I will plead guilty to reckless endangerment, be given a year's probation and assessments for court costs and probation-officer costs and costs to cover costs. At some random point over the next year, one time, I will be called upon to be drug-tested. It won't happen for almost a year, my very last week of probation. I'll pass it.

The sharper I get, the more it'll come into focus how far gone I was. What I never knew before is how low-grade fucked up I was day in and day out, all the time, whether I was drinking or using that day or not. I